Praise for Finding the Language of Grace

'*This tender book is not only intellectually sound, but also deeply emotionally literate... You are in for a treat.*'

Baroness Sheila Hollins

'*Abbot Christopher's gentle style and broad knowledge allow* Finding the Language of Grace *to serve as an approachable, practical companion in discovering how to articulate not only grace itself but the virtues that proceed from a deep understanding of grace in gratitude, deep love and most pertinently, hope.*'

Benedict Plimmer, *Catholic Student Network*

FINDING THE LANGUAGE OF GRACE

Rediscovering Transcendence

CHRISTOPHER JAMISON

BLOOMSBURY CONTINUUM
LONDON · OXFORD · NEW YORK · NEW DELHI · SYDNEY

BLOOMSBURY CONTINUUM
Bloomsbury Publishing Plc
50 Bedford Square, London, WC1B 3DP, UK
29 Earlsfort Terrace, Dublin 2, Ireland

BLOOMSBURY, BLOOMSBURY CONTINUUM and the Diana logo are trademarks
of Bloomsbury Publishing Plc

First published in Great Britain 2022

A catalogue record for this book is available from the British Library

Library of Congress Cataloguing-in-Publication data has been applied for

ISBN: TPB: 978-1-3994-0271-2; eBook: 978-1-3994-0270-5;
ePDF: 978-1-3994-0269-9

2 4 6 8 10 9 7 5 3 1

Typeset by Deanta Global Publishing Services, Chennai, India
Printed and bound in Great Britain by CPI Group (UK) Ltd, Croydon CR0 4YY

To find out more about our authors and books visit www.bloomsbury.com
and sign up for our newsletters

To Alda, Gordon and Jonathan, gracious friends

Contents

Acknowledgements

This book was a long time in coming. So first I want to thank Bloomsbury for keeping faith with me. In particular I thank my editor Robin Baird-Smith for persuading me to stay with the concept of this book, for giving me a new impetus to write and for supporting me throughout the writing process. Secondly, I thank several friends who read early drafts or sections of drafts, especially Peter Tyler, Austen Ivereigh and Ralph Townsend; unlike me, they all have doctorates and really know what they're talking about. I'm so grateful for their expertise and their time. Finally, I thank several organizations whose work has influenced the way I think and the way I live. Million Minutes is a Catholic youth charity that helps me and others understand how to accompany the young and the best language to use for such accompaniment. Their Courtyard Project is described in Chapter Three. CTVC is a media company I work with, specializing in the production of religious and ethical content across a range of media. Its wonderful staff help me to find the right language to communicate grace today. In collaboration with me and

Million Minutes, they were part of the AloneTogether team, a web-based project described in Chapter One.

Listening to the searing pain of those who survived sexual abuse by clergy, and participating in inquiries into these crimes, dominated my life during much of the time that immediately preceded the writing of this book. I acknowledge that their suffering has influenced my approach to the language of grace. I am deeply grateful for the conversations that so many survivors have had with me.

In the background while I have been writing has been the support of my Benedictine brethren and the kindness of the parish community of St Mary Moorfields, London, where I have been based during various lockdowns. Without such personal support I am unable to write, so I am grateful to them all for their unwitting contribution to this book.

Introduction

Grace is poured upon your lips.
Psalm 45.2

WHY TRANSCENDENCE?

There is a problem in our culture that we can barely speak about because the loss of the language to describe it *is* the problem. We are losing the ability to speak openly about fundamental aspects of our lives such as love and joy, beauty and goodness, or hatred and greed, anger and vanity. These experiences are what matter most to us, for good or for ill. We long for joy and beauty, we fear the destructive power of anger and greed. They are expressed physically, but they come from the realm of the transcendent, the dimension beyond the physical. Transcendence is the dimension that people find themselves unable to name.

The Irish poet and Nobel Laureate, Seamus Heaney (1939–2013), summarized the problem succinctly: 'The biggest change in my lifetime has been the evaporation of the transcendent from all our discourse.' Public language today has a focus that is almost exclusively commercial and practical: used to sell us something or to persuade us of something or to increase our technical understanding. This transactional language can engulf us so completely that many people find it difficult to speak publicly about the ultimate but mysterious dimensions of life. Those who do – the singers and the poets – stand out and are ever more sought after.

The challenge is to revitalize the language of transcendence for our present time. In the Christian tradition, the ultimate transcendent reality that people experience is grace, the action of God in the world. To give our search for the transcendent a focus, therefore, I'll concentrate on grace and on how Christian writers have described grace at work in their own lives or in the lives of their fictional characters. This means focusing on what I call *the language of grace*, a language that is handed on within the Christian tradition to be rediscovered afresh in every generation.

WHY THE LANGUAGE OF GRACE?

The language of grace is universal and everyone can learn to speak it, whether or not they have a formal religious faith. Grace is at work in everybody's life, irrespective of their creed, and many people who call themselves spiritual but not religious are often looking for their own version of the language of grace. For a Christian, the accepted terms that describe grace are found in the Church's liturgy and doctrine. These liturgical and doctrinal texts are the necessary infrastructure of Christian living, but they are not sufficient to capture all God's activity. Grace finds new expression in the daily lives of every generation of Christians, including expressions that stretch the formal language to its limits and beyond.

The awareness of grace as a lived experience and the use of language to express it have been eroded by two equal but opposite forces. On the one hand, we in Britain, for example, live in a society where, in the 2011 census, one quarter of the population reported they had 'no religion', a figure expected to have grown significantly when the 2021 census results are published. Historically religion has been the principal way for people to learn how to express their experience of transcendence. Religious faith today is rarely a family inheritance (even among those brought up in a faith community); it is mainly an adult choice by a minority of people. This means that the language which recognizes transcendence in human experience has died in the lives of many people; occasionally encountered in formal texts at weddings and funerals, it is no longer a living language through which people describe their own experience. The Mind, Body and Spirit section of bookshops offers a wide range of spiritual books, some diets are spoken of as having an almost mystical quality of purity and TV programmes on the natural world frequently offer a commentary that suggests the supernatural. Given that the transcendent is a real dimension of life, it's not surprising that, when the widely spoken language of grace dies out, there is an outbreak of local 'dialects of transcendence' within different groups. But the authors of spiritual systems, diet regimes and TV documentaries lack a common language.

For most people in Britain today, religious language has no meaning, and it has not been replaced by any generally accepted way of expressing the transcendent dimensions of life.

In reaction to this, there has on the other hand been a growth in religious fundamentalism, an attitude of some people of faith who have weaponized their community's religious language. Religious expressions other than the traditional language of creeds and doctrines are considered heretical. Failure to adhere strictly to every article of faith is judged to be the reason for our society's religious and moral decline. Such perceived laxity justifies condemnation and even expulsion from the faith community. In recent decades this fundamentalist tendency has grown in most major religions.

Between them, the decline of religion and the rise of fundamentalism have shrunk the space for describing the lived experience of grace. The language of grace is dying.

LANGUAGE: A PATHWAY TO GRACE

My own interest in languages stems from my family's history. We are a family with roots in Australia going back to the nineteenth century, and in the early 1950s my father was made managing director of an Australian company whose global HQ was in England. So, as a babe in arms, I emigrated to England with my family. Though a great deal of the company's business was done in mainland Europe, especially France, my father was astonished to find that hardly any of the HQ directors or managers spoke French. The French directors, by contrast, all spoke English. My father's professional surprise combined with the family's experience of our first summer holiday in England, a rainy fortnight in Frinton, a serious culture shock for an Australian family. Thereafter we went on holiday to France, and so began my father's campaign to ensure that his four sons all spoke French. Luckily, I had good French teachers at school who encouraged me to learn Spanish as well, culminating in a modern languages degree at university.

Two parts of that course proved personally significant. First, there was a unit on linguistics, the scientific and philosophical study of language, which explains how language is not only a communication tool but also part of what makes us human. I began to wonder how people have the ability to say things that have never been said before, and how people acquire that generative skill. Secondly, I had the chance to study French and Spanish literature for three years, with a strong focus on the novel. One category of European novels that appealed to me became known as the Catholic Novel. For example, in 1951 the English author Graham Greene wrote *The End of the Affair*, describing a typical love triangle, but with an added dimension: as the characters struggle with their failings there is a deep strand of grace running through their lives. Earlier in the twentieth century in France, in *Thérèse Desqueyroux*,

François Mauriac explored grace at work in the life of a woman who attempted to murder her cruel husband. These novelists wrote stories about faith and loss of faith, about sin and redemption, but not in a simplistic way. Rather, they often inverted those classic religious ideas and explored whether God was to be found outside such classic doctrinal categories. The God who is at work in these novels is not a power who intervenes to save the day, but rather a subtle presence, usually amid failure; in these stories, grace is a quality communicated through a luminous use of language. While I'd come across grace described in scripture and sermons, these novels showed grace at work in people's lives in unexpected ways. The authors were undoubtedly describing a divine presence without using the formal language of religion. This was for me an introduction to a new and deeply attractive language of grace.

LANGUAGE FOUR WAYS

A kind word at the right moment is remembered with gratitude, but a careless sentence can leave a long-lasting wound. The way people speak really matters; so does what people write. The same is true of listening: attentive listening to someone in distress calms anxieties. Even reading can be a gift to other people: reading well at a funeral, for example, brings consolation to the mourners. And a poem can be a moment of joy for the solitary reader. Speaking and writing, listening and reading: these four forms of language can be a means of communicating transcendence and grace.

In the coming chapters I will describe each form of language as a means of grace, as exemplified in a great writer. But first, in Chapter One, I offer a practical description of grace, showing how it fosters trust and inner freedom. Then in Chapter Two we meet the first of our great Christian writers, the twentieth-century Japanese novelist Shusaku Endo, and his novel *Silence*, in which listening is central. In Chapter Three, we move back to the medieval world and the legend of the Holy Grail, a story that highlights the importance of speaking well. In Chapter Four, Teresa of Avila and John of the Cross illustrate how the act of writing is a spiritual undertaking. Chapter Five features the contemporary American novelist Marilynne Robinson, and her fictional world of Gilead, a world of truths that we enter through the joy of reading her poetic prose. In the last chapter, we'll look at language that is beyond words, and try to read some challenging, contemporary situations in the light of what previous chapters have taught us.

All languages require practice. At the end of each chapter, therefore, there'll be an optional set of exercises for you to do at your own pace. This isn't a handbook or a user's manual, but I hope for you it can be a source book of inspiring texts, helping you to find transcendence and revitalize your own language of grace.

What is Grace?

Surely goodness and kindness will follow me all the days of my life.

Ps 23.6

MISTRUST: GRACELESS LIVING

In its 2018 report entitled *Truth Decay*, the Rand Corporation noted that 'Americans' reliance on facts to discuss public issues has declined significantly in the past two decades, leading to political paralysis and collapse of civil discourse.' This collapse is seen in the inability to listen to opposing arguments, for example, or even to accept scientific findings. All too often, this leads to aggressive verbal attacks on those with differing views. 'The study cites the immigration debate as a present-day example of the erosion of civil discourse,' states the official summary of the report:

> Without agreement on a common set of facts about the number of immigrants entering the

US, their economic costs and contributions, and
the amount of crime they do or do not commit,
it becomes difficult to have important policy
debates and come to policy solutions.

Even worse is the ease with which anybody can publish
what they like via social media. Until recently, the
aggressive and demeaning comments made about
people online would never have found a publisher to
print them. Now they are sent around the world in an
instant.

The decline in public discourse and how we might
counteract it is the background to this book but not
its theme. The belligerent tone of public conversations
is often founded on a deep mistrust of institutions and
individuals. What are the roots of this mistrust? In
my experience, those roots are closer to home than we
might want to admit.

What's your earliest memory in life? Mine is the
memory of being lost on a beach. My family was visiting
Melbourne, our home town and the place of my birth,
the city we had left when I was a babe in arms. When I
was nearly five years old, in December 1956, the whole
family returned by plane for our first visit home since
leaving. At that time flying such a distance was itself an
adventure, an adventure heightened by my father's war
stories as a former navigator in the RAAF. We arrived in
the height of the Australian summer, just in time for the
Melbourne Olympics. The travellers' tales of those days
are not real memories of mine, however, but stories the
family has rehearsed ever since, legends shared between

us. My overriding memory of that trip is being lost on a beach in Brighton, the Melbourne suburb where I was born. I remember it was a beautiful summer's day, but that I was in tears because I couldn't find my family; I'd wandered off along the seashore and got lost in the crowd. A kind woman saw me crying and took me to a policeman (I still remember his white pith helmet) who then walked me back along the beach to find my family. They hadn't been that far away, but I had panicked at this first experience of separation. This memory of my five-year-old self is still quite vivid in my mind, as is the emotion of being lost.

In my work as a priest and monk that began about 20 years after that experience, I was learning how to lead retreats, especially retreats for young people. As part of that work, I asked people to think about their earliest memories and to share them with the group if they wanted to. Time and again people described an experience of separation and isolation. Not an experience of love, but an experience of losing love. Of course, loss presumes there was something to lose in the first place, but the love isn't the first memory: for many people their original memory is the *loss* of love. Why are the negative experiences of loss and isolation so often people's strongest early memories?

One striking account of early memory comes from the award-winning actor, Tom Hanks. During his 2016 appearance on BBC Radio 4's long running series *Desert Island Discs* he was asked by the presenter, Kirsty Young, to talk about his teenage self. 'I started asking myself a whole different set of questions,' he said.

'And what were they?' asked Young.

Hanks hesitated. 'Those questions were: how do I find the vocabulary for what's rattling around inside my head?'

Young pursued this: 'Are you able to articulate those feelings?'

Hanks then welled up, couldn't speak. Eventually he said, 'What have you done to me, Kirsty?' followed by a nervous laugh and, finally, 'What it was, it was the vocabulary of loneliness.' Hanks then described his 20-year-old self being cast in a Chekhov play and the director saying, 'All the great plays are about loneliness.' That phrase hit him like a lightning bolt: he realized that was why he was in the theatre – to overcome his loneliness – but his 15-year-old self hadn't had the vocabulary to express that.

I want to look at the possibility that such memories of isolation are also a person's first actual experience of what the Christian tradition calls original sin. If loneliness and mistrust are a fundamental human experience, then this is a place that the language of grace must explore, and that exploration will try to find the right words to restore trust so that love can flourish. This will involve looking at mistrust head on and even getting inside it. As will become clear, the language of grace will include describing the absence of grace. This encounter between light and darkness is disconcerting, even frightening, but cannot be avoided if the language of grace is going to touch real life. That confrontation in people's lives is a compelling area of exploration for writers and artists.

Over the course of the twentieth century, as modern attitudes rebelled against the idea of inherited wickedness, original sin got a bad press. The great fourth-century theologian St Augustine did indeed believe that the sin of Adam was passed on to children by the sexual act of their parents. But while this way of expressing original sin was widespread, it has never had the formal approval of the Catholic Church. I believe that my childhood experience (and the earliest experience of many others, as I discovered) offers an alternative insight into what the Christian tradition means by original sin.

Put simply, when people realize that they are alone, they find they have a basic instinct to be mistrustful. Looked at in this light, my day at the beach was when I discovered that my family couldn't be relied on to be there the whole time, especially if I chose simply to wander off! This realization was an end of innocence, and the start of that tendency to weigh up situations, make judgements about people and choose whether to trust them. At one level that was a necessary part of growing up and keeping safe; but it was also the first time I realized my inherent aloneness and my mistrust of others.

People are born with a sense of being alone: babies cry when they're hungry, perhaps because they don't trust anybody to attend to their needs unless there is an immediate response. Good childhood experiences, especially good family experiences, create strong bonds and enable young people to love others trustingly. In a normal home, infants come to know that they will be cared for, and as a result trust their parents. Bad childhood experiences, especially abuse, lock a person into mistrust, sometimes for life. My recent meetings with those abused by clergy and teachers have revealed to me just how devastating and long-lasting such experiences are. Mistrust is powerfully amplified by abuse. Some survivors have shown heroic generosity by trusting me and other church leaders enough to meet with us so we can understand their experiences and work more effectively to protect children. Many survivors of clergy abuse will understandably never again trust any priest and want no further contact with the Church.

Original mistrust explains why a common first memory is the moment when we realize for the first time the full force of being alone in the world. Ever since that day I first discovered I was lost and alone, my whole life has been a quest to overcome my original mistrust.

This is no simplistic claim. It was my privilege to be at a conference in Dublin in 1998, addressed by a woman who would become President of Ireland, Mary McAleese. Ms McAleese is from Northern Ireland and was the first Catholic to be Vice-Chancellor of Queen's University Belfast; the clue as to why this is notable is in the university's name and the historical struggle of Catholic republicans against the Crown. In her address to the conference of British and Irish head teachers, Ms McAleese challenged the notion that the aim of education is to foster lifelong learning. Her own life and the life of modern Ireland showed, she said, that progress also required lifelong *unlearning*, above all unlearning mistrust. The Good Friday Agreement had been signed just a few months earlier, offering a chance to end Ireland's troubles, but when communities have murdered each other for centuries, she went on, the depth of mistrust is so great that the unlearning must be actively and carefully promoted. That evening, at the dinner in her honour, I found myself sitting next to an Irish guest. At the end of the dinner, the conference chairman, an Englishman, invited us to stand for the loyal toast: 'the President of the Republic of Ireland'. As we sat down, I commented to my Irish neighbour that it was good to hear an Englishman toasting the Irish Head of State.

'Up to a point', came his reply. 'An Irishman would have toasted the President of Ireland.'

The need for unlearning mistrust applies to so many areas of life. The theology of original sin is the simple statement that human beings will constantly be undermined by their inability to trust, and so must take intentional steps to overcome it. Mistrust can be diminished but never removed completely, so that even on their deathbed many a saint has experienced the arrival of the demons of infidelity and hopelessness.

This whole process of mistrust is well illustrated in the legend from which the notion of original sin is drawn, the story of Adam and Eve. This is one of the truest stories I know, provided we understand that the truths being communicated are not scientific truths but truths about the way humans behave.

In the opening chapters of the Book of Genesis, the storyteller describes God creating the universe, culminating in the creation of man and woman. The couple are given permission to name everything in the universe and the privilege of living in paradise: all the fruits of the earth will be theirs and all the animals will serve them. God asks only one thing: Adam and Eve mustn't eat of the fruit of one tree, the tree of the knowledge of good and evil. The fruit of that tree can't be eaten because, as the serpent in the story says quite correctly, if they know how to judge good and evil then they themselves will have become as gods. But what the serpent doesn't tell them is that because there is only one God, to eat of the tree will put them in conflict with the true God. They will no longer trust God's judgement but will seek their own.

But Adam and Eve do go and eat the fruit, and afterwards they do indeed begin to make their own judgements. The first such judgement is to see themselves as naked, and so they clothe themselves. Adam and Eve have become self-conscious, no longer trusting themselves to appear as they really are. This is the first sign of the collapse of trust. Then in the evening the Lord God takes a walk in his beautiful paradise garden, but when they hear God coming, Adam and Eve hide. When God finds them, Adam tells God, 'I was afraid because I was naked, so I hid.' Adam's self-consciousness leads to a collapse of trust not only in himself but also in God, from whom he now wants to hide. Not content with mistrusting God, Adam then turns on Eve and blames her for the sin of eating the forbidden fruit, thus destroying the trust between them.

In this short story trust collapses like a row of dominoes: Adam doesn't trust his naked self, so he fears God isn't trustworthy either, and finally he no longer trusts Eve. Mistrust of self, God and others is of a piece. This is original sin, the inability to trust combined with the increasing isolation that mistrust breeds. The Adam and Eve story involves fear and shame, but the fundamental reality that causes these emotions is mistrust. In contrast to the pagan creation stories that see the cosmos as a battlefield between good and evil, the Hebrew belief is that God has created a good, well-ordered universe yet there is evil within it. The explanation of evil offered by Genesis is that people don't trust the goodness of God and his world so they turn in on themselves, ultimately finding they can't even trust themselves. The rest of the Bible shows God at work to save people from their mistrust and isolation.

As became clear during the pandemic lockdowns, isolation is a life-threatening situation that requires us to work continuously to protect vulnerable people from its effects. Language is a key part of the way society does this, through speaking to those living on their own, writing to them and even reading to or with them. This is the language of grace as social action.

Secular society has rejected biblical insights about original sin and instead has rushed to an alternative, the belief that human beings are perfectible. If there is no fundamental flaw, then we can set about organizing things to remove the barriers to perfectibility. What replaced the notion of original sin in the twentieth century was a new optimism that, with the help of modern developments such as science and technology, psychology and economics, humanity could now begin curing human flaws to bring about a perfect society.

Such an optimistic vision is the characteristic that unites both Fascism and Marxism, using both terms in their historical sense. These movements were popular: Hitler and Mussolini both won democratic elections and Marxist revolutions gained widespread support. These political philosophies promised to fix society through the proper management of the economy and politics, to rid the world of all obstacles to progress, including those people who constituted obstacles. The loss of a sense of humanity's original sin underwrote many of the twentieth century's greatest acts of violence, be it Nazism's Final Solution, Stalin's purges or the industrial policies of Chairman Mao that caused widespread famine.

In reaction to these abusive regimes, the desire to establish human rights in law became one of the late-twentieth century's greatest projects. The whole concept of human rights is based on a transcendent understanding of the world: you cannot physically see a right. Yet how to express these unseen rights remains highly disputed and the language around them is far from settled. For example, some people in Britain want to remove the European Convention on Human Rights from UK law and substitute it with a British Bill of Rights.

In spite of the successful establishment of human rights in many countries, the scale of the twentieth century's great acts of violence is such that, in modern times, mistrust has grown. By and large, we began the twenty-first century mistrusting ideas and institutions that offer big solutions to society's problems. Membership of political parties, trade unions and churches all shrank dramatically in the UK towards the end of the last century, with political party membership showing the most marked decline. Yet climate change and the Covid-19 pandemic require global political solutions if lives are to be saved. Anti-vax activism is based on systematic mistrust of scientists and methodically undermines public health programmes to contain the pandemic by describing public health measures as schemes designed to harm us. In a very different tone of voice, vaccination hesitancy is uncertainty among some groups about who to trust, often based on past abuse of their ethnic community. Whether based on obsessive conspiracy theories or on reasonable hesitation, lack of trust materially reduces society's success in addressing issues of life and death.

If the language of grace describes how mistrust is overcome, then it has a significant part to play in re-establishing confidence in leaders and institutions. The absence of such confidence was played out in the grotesque scenes of violent assault on the US Congress in January 2021. Convinced that the country was run by a corrupt elite who rigged the general election, this angry mob took mistrust of leaders and institutions to new levels of expression in a stable Western democracy. Yet these are the very leaders and institutions that will have to be trusted if we are to address the world's current challenges.

GRACE: TRUST RESTORED

Grace is God's way of restoring our trust in the goodness of life. The relationship between goodness and grace can perhaps be understood by analogy with food. If food is nourishing, then it's considered to be full of goodness. Similarly, grace is a goodness that nourishes the soul; it feeds the good in us so that we can trust each other and flourish together.

Grace is not a thing, however; it's not another item in the world that I can acquire. It is a quality, not a substance. In everyday language this quality is expressed in several ways. When we say somebody has 'fallen from grace' we mean they are no longer appreciated. So grace is, first, the quality of being appreciated, the experience that affirms my goodness. Secondly, we add the indefinite article *a*, as in 'a grace', to mean a specific experience of goodness. For example, a guest might say. 'It's been a real grace to live with your family.' Finally, grace means the act of giving thanks, as seen in *gratitude*, a word derived from grace. Gratitude responds to and multiplies grace. Thomas Aquinas, whose writings are a touchstone of Catholic theology, notes that these three aspects of grace have a logical sequence: the underlying grace of love is the necessary condition for giving somebody a particular grace, and gratitude is the consequence of this gift. This sequence is found in the lives of those people who manifest the quality we call grace.

Some common expressions can illustrate this further.

For what we are about to receive may the Lord make us truly grateful.

Grace before meals, such as the one quoted here, is a simple but powerful expression of thanking God for the food that sustains life. Habitual gratitude for being alive is the most basic way to sustain the goodness of life; to keep giving thanks in the midst of life's trials is to be on the way to overcoming them.

There but for the grace of God go I.

A phrase such as this one acknowledges that the grace of God acts in my life to make me a better person. Grace sometimes comes through specific events, when life takes a particular turn for the better, an actual experience of grace overcoming something negative and restoring life's goodness.

May the grace of our Lord Jesus Christ and the love of God and the fellowship of the Holy Spirit be with us all.

In the Christian tradition, we speak of the grace of God as the continuing work of Christ in the world. In creation God brings life from nothing, the first grace offered to us. In Christ's redeeming work, Christians believe that God brings new life from the nothingness of sin, the second grace. The prayer quoted here is known simply as 'the Grace'; it acknowledges the Christ-dimension in the lives of those present. All Church services are basically ways of opening the hearts and minds of those present to receive this grace.

Grace is not simply trying harder to be good, however; it's not the same as virtue. It operates in our lives and invites us to co-operate. As we'll see later, grace works in the lives of flawed human beings despite themselves. Similarly, the crucifixion of Jesus is understood by Christians to be both a great evil and a moment of grace. Grace is the quality that transforms lives even in their darkest moments.

Grace may confer on us comfort and consolation or reconciliation and reassurance; it may also bring in some way a deeper level of understanding and acceptance of reality. Or it can take the form of disruption or shock, as we find in the stories of the American Catholic novelist Flannery O'Connor (1925–64), who employed grotesqueness and violence in her stories to illustrate the workings of grace on her characters. She explained her fictional language of grace as follows: 'I have found that violence is strangely capable of returning my characters to reality and preparing them to accept their moment of grace. Their heads are so hard that almost nothing else will work.'

Gratitude is the human response to all these dimensions of grace. Gratitude for life and food. Saying 'thank God' for a particular turn of events, even, with hindsight, for painful events. Finally, Eucharist is the Greek word for thanksgiving, and the ancient name for Mass or Holy Communion, the high point of Christian worship.

The opposite of gratitude for the gift of life is to see life as a catastrophe, be it a catastrophe currently underway or a catastrophe about to happen. The choice we make each morning is either to give thanks for the new day or to catastrophize it. Even a relaxed 'I'll take this day as it comes' is to choose a downbeat form of gratitude. This choice became a very existential one during the pandemic lockdowns. There was indeed a catastrophe unfolding everywhere, in the local neighbourhood and in the wider world. It would be understandable, then, to begin the day by rehearsing all the difficulties of what might lie ahead: possible redundancy, sick and dying relatives, children to be home schooled. That instinctive reaction led many of us to experience significant depression and mental illness.

During the early days of the pandemic, I helped create www.alonetogether.org.uk, a website offering spiritual help to those facing the new challenges of lockdown. One of the insights we offered was to begin each day with a quiet time of gratitude for simply being alive, setting aside the day's problems just for a moment to focus on what will be the good things today. This daily practice is not running away from the difficulties, but rather building a positive foundation on which to face them. Within a month, 10,000 unique visitors had accessed the site, many writing to us saying how much the resources were helping them. It's still available, and people continue to find it helpful.

We can find the quality of grace in life every day by a simple act of gratitude. This is not just grace before meals: this is grace before life. Connecting this to the understanding of mistrust described in the previous section, to be grateful is to trust life and to catastrophize is to mistrust life. The challenge for us today is to trust that life has a meaning beyond the daily struggle to survive, and to recognize that we are free to embrace or reject that meaning.

In previous eras, the great question was, 'What is there in the world?' The quest was to understand what the world is made of and how it works. As Christian thinkers described what they knew about the material world, they included grace as part of it, part of the stuff of life. Grace was understood in the popular mind as something infused into people, like a blood transfusion. The quest for knowledge culminated in the scientific revolutions of the modern era, which have succeeded in giving a credible description of the material world and its processes. While that quest continues and may yet contain surprises, it has been answered so well that it is no longer the big question. The question that haunts the modern mind is 'Why?' *Why* does the world exist? The 'why' is now a more urgent question than the 'what'. In this new context, the idea of grace as an infusion is no longer what strikes people; more striking now is to see grace as the answer to the question why life exists, the meaning of life that gets us out of bed every morning.

The Dominican theologian Cornelius Ernst explored this theme in his book on grace, and memorably wrote: 'Meaning is that process by which the world to which we belong becomes the world that belongs to us.' From this perspective, people are not just items in the world alongside other forms of life; instead, people are the reason the world exists. Note 'belongs to us', not 'to me'. This is a shared meaning through which we learn to trust each other as we work together in the world: how to build good communities, how to do business fairly, how to explain things to each other when we disagree. These day-to-day actions are the building blocks of life's wider purpose, the task of trust building.

Ernst describes God as 'the meaning of meaning' that everybody longs for; we have a longing to reach out beyond ourselves, not only to love others but also to find a purpose beyond everyday life. This is a longing to be connected to God, to enjoy loving communion with the source of love. The language of grace is the pathway to this, a pathway discovered by many people but especially by writers and artists. Within this wider, divine meaning we all have a destiny, a personal meaning, which we need to discover and then choose freely to embrace. I get out of bed every morning because my life has meaning. Writers and artists can make this experience come alive in a unique way; their contribution is not an optional extra but a basic resource in showing the grace of meaning in our lives. This is, however, where the language of grace encounters opposition from a contemporary language that denies both that life has meaning and that people possess the inner freedom to choose that meaning.

'OUR MINDS ARE NOT OUR OWN'

There are many strong voices that subvert the assumption that there's a purpose to life other than the struggle to survive. They do this by denying that people are free to choose their purpose through, for example, acts of love and kindness. Neo-Darwinian attitudes, Freudian sexual theory and Marxist economics came together in the last century to leave twenty-first-century men and women stripped of their mental freedom. The American novelist Marilynne Robinson sums up Neo-Darwinism and meme theory (more about this in a moment) as having one major consequence: 'both of them represent the mind as a passive conduit of purposes other than those the mind ascribes to itself. It reiterates that essential modernist position, that our minds are not our own.'

Modernity has indeed set people free in many ways, through democracy and economic development, through medical science and technology. But the interior world, the human soul, has ended up as a part of life that modernity says is controlled by everything except itself. It's either genes or parents or the marketplace that shape our behaviour. This undermines our readiness to take responsibility for our lives. A particular and very dominant scientific philosophy has succeeded in creating a popular new assumption, that our minds are not our own, without ever making an outright declaration of it. We could be excused for not noticing that this is the implication of what some scientists are telling us. While shaking off religion in the name of freedom, many of us may unwittingly embrace a philosophy that takes away spiritual freedom.

Meme theory is a good example of this attitude. Memes are to the mind, goes the theory, what genes are to the body, namely the inherited components that make up our mental world just as genes are the inherited components that make up our bodies. Darwin observed that species mutate randomly and concluded that the fittest mutants would survive and others die out. But he couldn't explain how such mutation happened. Gene theory has since explained how the genes we inherit can mutate randomly.

The discovery of genes has given new wind to evolutionary theories and has fostered the rise of neo-Darwinian science. The survival of the fittest explains all human development, say the neo-Darwinians, not only the development of the human body but also the development of human culture. The gift-giving of humans, for example, like all benevolence, is seen as a meme: we think we are controlling the act of giving a gift to a loved one but actually the idea or meme of gift-giving is controlling us. Our apparent generosity is nothing of the sort; it is an inherited custom that supports the survival of the species. Human freedom is diminished as even benevolence is no longer seen as a free act.

The celebrated American biologist Stephen Jay Gould (1941–2002) cautioned against pressing the claims of Darwinism too far. 'Virtually all thinking people accept the factuality of evolution,' he wrote in the *New York Review of Books* in 1997,

> and no conclusion in science enjoys better documentation ... The radicalism of natural selection lies in its power to dethrone some of the deepest and most traditional comforts of Western thought ... Richard Dawkins would narrow the focus of explanation even one step further – to genes struggling for reproductive success within passive bodies (organisms) under the control of genes – a hyper-Darwinian idea that I regard as a logically flawed and basically foolish caricature of Darwin's genuinely radical intent.

A similar denial of freedom is at work in Marxist economics. Any owner of a business is by definition oppressing those he employs, and no amount of benevolence towards employees can change this. The overthrow of capitalism is inevitable, as the workers will rise up to seize control. No amount of avoiding action can prevent this, because the economic structure dictates everything.

Or take Freud's theories of sexuality. Freud believed that any expression of spirituality in art or culture was an expression of repressed sexuality; Jung challenged this theory, saying it implied that culture was a mere farce, the morbid consequence of repressed sexuality. 'Yes, so it is,' was Freud's reply.

Such powerful voices tell us that our natural understanding of our actions is false. We are not people free to love: we're simply nature's survivors, or economic entities, or sexual animals. Without question, such scientific, economic and psychological discoveries do contain significant insights about life that are of great benefit. Yet some claims based on these discoveries go beyond the boundaries of their science and seek to explain the whole of life. The challenge we face is how to contain these important scientific discoveries. They need to be contextualized within a broader understanding which allows that life may have a higher purpose, and that people have real inner freedom to pursue that purpose. The language of grace is the language that provides this broader understanding.

What we need is a dialogue between the language of the sciences and the language of grace. This is not a debate between competing explanations of life where one side is trying to win an argument, sweeping away all other insights except their own. Instead, this dialogue is a process to which many people from diverse disciplines can contribute, and have their contributions respected.

RECLAIMING OUR MINDS

Such a model of dialogue exists in the events sponsored by the Templeton Foundation, where scientists, philosophers and theologians meet regularly, with intellectual humility paramount. The foundation is best known for the Templeton Prize, one of the world's largest annual individual awards, awarded to those 'whose exemplary achievements advance Sir John Templeton's philanthropic vision: harnessing the power of the sciences to explore the deepest questions of the universe and humankind's place and purpose within it'. In 2020, the Prize was awarded to Francis Crick, the former Director of the Human Genome Project responsible for advancing our understanding of genes. 'He has demonstrated how religious faith can motivate and inspire rigorous scientific research,' reads the award's citation. 'He endeavours to encourage religious communities to embrace the latest discoveries of genetics and the biomedical sciences as insights to enrich and enlarge their faith.'

Another strand of the Foundation's work is called the Humble Approach Initiative; within this strand in 2014, it explored 'a new approach to prayer and the brain', taking as its starting point the work of Dr Iain McGilchrist as set out in his book *The Master and His Emissary: The Divided Brain and the Making of the Western World.* 'This quite remarkable book will radically change the way you understand the world and yourself,' claimed the reviewer in *Scientific and Medical Network Review.*

McGilchrist is a former consultant psychiatrist who has done research in neuroimaging, and has also been a Fellow of All Souls, Oxford, where he undertook research in English literature and the principles of literary criticism. He unites many disciplines, so it's worth staying with him for a while to understand how he expands the space in which the language of grace can be used and respected. The research findings that McGilchrist presents centre on something known about the brain for well over a century: its two hemispheres control different human functions. For example, in general terms, the left hemisphere (LH) controls the right-hand side of the body, and the right hemisphere (RH) controls the left-hand side of the body. In addition, LH controls more logical and systematic functions, and RH is seen as the more creative and empathetic side of the brain.

The essence of McGilchrist's thesis is that the brain's dominant mode of operation is not LH's capacity for precise analysis of information but RH's capacity for imprecise understanding of whole entities, especially living beings. His sweeping account is based on research found in some 2,500 scientific papers, scrupulously sourced and cited in the copious endnotes.

The example that for me illuminates his central point most clearly is a series of line drawings of a tree done by the same subject in three ways: first, under normal conditions (a drawing of a whole tree); secondly, with only LH active (a detailed drawing of the right half of the tree); and thirdly, with only RH active (a poor drawing of the whole tree.) I concluded that LH knows a great deal about half of the tree, while RH knows something about the whole tree. RH is fundamental to our knowledge of the world, but – because it is a little blurry – humans often neglect or sideline it.

McGilchrist makes the LH/RH divide the basis for a critique of modern culture, which, he suggests, has over-privileged the analytic form of knowing of LH almost to the exclusion of other forms of human knowing. The result is a culture that knows a lot about half of reality, and which has unwittingly created an environment that fosters mental illness, because whole areas of life are denied, or at best denigrated, as simply a matter of taste or opinion with no 'knowledge' content.

McGilchrist worries about the increased incidence of schizophrenia, which he claims is an illness unique to modern times. While ancient Greek physicians describe many kinds of mental illness, such as depression, there is, he claims, no recorded incidence of schizophrenia till relatively recently. According to McGilchrist's controversial position, in a person suffering from schizophrenia, the rationality of LH has come to completely dominate a person's life, and RH plays little or no role in it. He or she has come to live in a private world detached from reality, which the subject nevertheless insists is completely rational. In such a mind, obsessions and conspiracy theories abound.

To explain how this imbalance has come about, McGilchrist begins with an analysis of human desires, which he divides into wants and longings. When we *want* something, we desire to possess it. When we *long* for something, we desire to be possessed by it. So, for example, I want to possess food, but I long to be held by my spouse. Even our language makes the distinction clear: real love is a desire to 'be-long' to another, not to 'possess' another. McGilchrist sees wanting as an LH function, a precise analysis of needs, while longing is an RH function, a sense of belonging to people. Consumer culture constantly stirs up our wants; as a result, we neglect our deeper longings. On this view, the transcendent dimension of life is unknown to LH, and since RH's insights are undervalued, our culture disallows the transcendent as a source of knowledge.

A classic question of cultural history is, why did the Scientific Revolution occur in the West in the modern era, and not in China or medieval Islam or medieval Europe? McGilchrist stands this on its head. He puts a very different question: How has it come about in the West that the only sort of knowledge taken seriously is scientific knowledge? In other societies and cultures where there have been major scientific advances, science is just one of several aspects of life. It is not regarded as more valuable or important than any other activity, as the only thing that 'really matters'. By contrast, in the West, there is unchecked, acquisitive science. It increasingly commands all society's energy and resources.

The growth of science to this position in Western culture is anomalous and exceptional. McGilchrist traces how a LH/RH balance was maintained in the West until it was finally swept away by the triumph of literalism over metaphor that began with the Enlightenment. Metaphor came increasingly to be a mere linguistic ornament, and not an important way of thinking about and interacting with the world. He concludes that this 'loss of metaphor is a loss of cognitive content'. If only science can know anything, swathes of human knowing are lost.

Neuroscience is telling us that it is not only unhealthy but unscientific for human beings to see themselves purely as analytic beings, who must think their way to personal authenticity. The good news is that there are ways of reversing this trend, and developing the language of grace is one of them.

Among recent Templeton Prize winners is Professor Freeman Dyson, who died in 2020. A leading British physicist, he was the son of an acclaimed church musician, Sir George Dyson. Speaking at a Templeton event in 2012, Professor Dyson explained that 'to understand the universe in a deep sense, minds count more than galaxies and planets ... We have more to learn from the poets than from the scientists when it comes to problems of the purpose of the universe.' To him, the insights of poets and creative writers of all kinds were intrinsic to his formidable intellectual grasp of reality. So it is to them that, in the following chapters, we now turn.

LANGUAGE EXERCISES

Gratitude

- For a month, take time each morning (maybe five or ten minutes) simply to give thanks for being alive. Name to yourself the good things in your life: the people, good memories, present blessings, future possibilities. Then look more broadly, giving thanks for the local community, for those dedicated to supporting others. More widely still, give thanks for the world, for its grace and beauty.
- If you are a person of faith, give thanks for the spirit of God present in your life and in the world. Read Psalm 95 (94 in some editions), a prayer of thanks and praise.
- At the end of the month, talk to someone you trust about how this gratitude exercise has left you feeling.

2

Listening

No speech, no word, no voice is heard, yet their
span extends through all the earth.

Psalm 19

WHAT IS LANGUAGE?

'The Only Speaker of his Tongue' is a short story written in 1985 by the Australian author David Malouf. He imagines a language expert ('a lexicographer') meeting the last living speaker of one of Australia's many native languages. 'When I think of my tongue being no longer alive in the mouths of men', observes the expert, 'a chill goes over me that is deeper than my own death, since it is the gathered death of all my kind.' Language is not only the passing on of bundles of information: it also carries the huge cultural inheritance 'of all my kind'. The expert explains how language passes on culture, concluding that

All this is a mystery. It is a mystery of the deep
past, but also of now. We recapture on our
tongue, when we first grasp the sound and
make it, the same word in the mouths of our
long dead fathers, whose blood we move in and
whose blood still moves in us. Language *is* that
blood.

Grace could be described as the lifeblood of Christianity,
the blood we move in and which still moves in us.
Given the central Christian doctrine of Christ's blood
shed for the redemption of the world, this seems an
apt metaphor to describe grace. Stretching Malouf's
understanding of language to its limits and adapting
it, I want to say, 'Language *is* that grace.' I'm not
saying the reverse, that grace is *only* language; there
are other, even stronger forms of grace – the grace of
the sacraments, for example. But good language *is* a
powerful vehicle of grace. This book is about the power
of *the language* of grace.

    There are so many ways to describe language that
it's doubtful one definition can encompass all those
activities which can be called 'language': body language,
sign language, dead languages, bird calls, to name but
a few. But Malouf's fictitious lexicographer gives us
a good insight into how language functions at a very
basic level. It is a sound that we first grasp and then
reproduce on our tongue. We listen to a sound and
then we speak 'the words, the great system of sound and
silence', as he describes it. Sound and silence that enable
an entire culture to function; a whole understanding

of life and death is sustained by those sounds and that silence. Language can convey grace because the way people speak includes a whole way of approaching life and death.

Animals too make sounds that carry meaning and sustain their culture: birdsong, mating calls, even laughter among some primates. But as far as we know the ability to speak completely new sentences and to generate new meanings is unique to humans. This language generation capacity is a significant example of the personal, interior freedom that marks us out from other beings. Human beings are the beings who are free to speak as they choose.

This skill also applies to the language of grace, which is above all 'a mystery of the deep past, but also of now'. It enables people to 'recapture on our tongue' the gracious insights of 'all my kind', to experience them and to pass them on. Like all languages, it begins with listening to 'the great system of sound and silence'. In our current Western culture, silence is not easily embraced, but when it is, then we can be surprised by the grace it conveys. So that is where this guide to the language of grace must begin, with listening to the language of silence.

SILENCE: SHUSAKU ENDO

Silence is a novel written in 1966 by the Japanese writer Shusaku Endo (1923–96). He was a prolific and internationally celebrated author; the English writer Graham Greene admired him to the extent that he wrote to him that 'Silence is so much better than my own *Power and Glory*.' Both novels describe the struggles of a Catholic priest in a time of persecution: Greene's in 1930s Mexico, and Endo's in seventeenth-century Japan. Recent acclaim for *Silence* has come from the Hollywood producer Martin Scorsese, who in 2016 made the book into a film.

Endo was baptised into the Catholic Church at the age of 12, and later described his baptism as putting on 'a ready-made suit, a Western suit, ill-matched to his Japanese body'. He spent most of his adult life struggling to understand the faith he inherited from his mother and whether it was compatible with Japanese culture. 'It seems to me that Catholicism is not a solo but a symphony,' he reflected.

> If I have trust in Catholicism it is because I
> find in it much more possibility than in any
> other religion for presenting the full symphony
> of humanity. The other religions have almost
> no fullness; they have but solo parts. Only
> Catholicism can present the full symphony.
> And unless there is in that symphony a part that
> corresponds to the mud swamp that is Japan, it
> cannot be true religion. What exactly that part is,
> that is what I want to find out.

His novels and short stories are his attempt to find that part of Catholic faith which corresponds to the mud swamp, an image he frequently used to describe Japan. He wants to find the place where grace and sin interact, and then depict an authentic religious faith in that place. For Endo, that interaction is found especially in the persecution of Japanese Christians during the seventeenth century, and specifically in one well-established historical fact: the leader of the Jesuit mission to Japan, Father Ferreira, committed apostasy – that is, renounced his faith. It is presumed that his apostasy was the result of torture, but nothing is known about the circumstances.

The historical background *is* known, however. The persecution of Christians was widespread; the public spectacle of their courage in the face of martyrdom was increasing rather than diminishing the number of converts, to the point where they were no longer simply executed. Instead, the authorities tortured Christians by suspending them upside down over a pit of excrement, carefully cutting open their head to reduce the blood pressure so they would stay alive longer and then slowly bleed to death. To escape this hideous death, the Christian had to walk on an image of Christ that the magistrate placed before them, an image known in Japanese as *fumi-e* (literally, the stepping-on picture). A few rare examples of *fumi-e* still exist, and the features of the bas-relief image are worn flat, presumably by the many feet that walked on it.

Around these facts, Endo weaves the compelling fiction of Father Rodrigues and Father Garrpe, Jesuit priests sent to Japan to find Ferreira. *Silence* describes the physical and spiritual journey of Rodrigues through his imagined letters home and reports. After narrowly escaping capture by the authorities, Garrpe and he decide to go in different directions, so Rodrigues finds himself on his own when he is eventually taken prisoner, betrayed by his Catholic servant, Kichijiro. He finally meets Ferreira, a shadow of his former self, now writing a book in Japanese to refute the claims of Christianity. Ferreira bears the scar of the slow bleeding, but it is not the torture that has defeated him but the impossibility of Christianity taking root in Japan. 'This country is a swamp,' he says, using Endo's favourite image for Japan. 'Whenever you plant a sapling in this swamp the roots begin to rot ... We have planted the sapling of Christianity in this swamp.'

Rodrigues is worn down not by being tortured himself but by hearing from his prison cell the groans of the Japanese Christians suspended over the pit. He is told that they have apostatized but will not be saved until he, Rodrigues, apostatizes as well. He gives in: 'I, too, stood on the sacred image ... Even now that face is looking at me with eyes of pity from the plaque rubbed flat by many feet. "Trample!" said those compassionate eyes. "Trample!"' In his reflections, he challenges God: 'Lord, I resented your silence.' Comes the reply: 'I was not silent. I suffered beside you.'

There then follows a dialogue with the Lord about Judas echoing the role of Kichijiro. In a final twist, the servant wants to confess his betrayal to the apostate priest he betrayed so that he can receive absolution. Rodrigues' final reflection is the conclusion of the book: 'Even now I am the last priest in this land. But our Lord was not silent. Even if he had been silent, my life until this day would have spoken of him.'

There are many layers of grace in this story, including the formal, sacramental grace of confession administered by an apostate priest. The heart of the novel, however, is the silence of the title, which is the silence of God in the face of suffering. And the climax is the once enthusiastic missionary trampling on the image of Christ but later imagining that Christ wanted him to do this.

The crisis of faith in the face of suffering is a timeless challenge. Endo's response to this challenge is not to ask 'why' – why is this happening – but 'where': where is God when people suffer, and why is he silent? Where is the grace in the suffering? The formal explanation of this question is known as 'theodicy', the justification of an all-powerful God's goodness in the face of human suffering. There are some intellectually adequate theodicies to be found in the textbooks, but they are coldly rational and not very compelling. Conversely, I find Endo's theodicy compelling but not very rational.

What is compelling is Endo's description of divine silence in the face of suffering combined with human shame at the inability to keep faith with God. This *feels* a very realistic description of what happens in the interaction between God and people in the midst of their suffering. Questioning God can lead to doubting the existence of God, but it can also lead to a deeper understanding of faith. Rodrigues still sees himself as 'the last priest', and acknowledges that, even if God had been silent, his life 'would have spoken of him'. Even his despair at God's silence has somehow been transformed. The same is true of the Judas in the story, Kichijiro. A friend who read this book told me how the account of

his betrayal was so compelling in its description of evil
that she was deeply disturbed by it. This thoroughly
loathsome character, the epitome of human corruption –
even he seeks divine forgiveness, another layer of grace
in this remarkable novel.

Somehow in the telling of all this Endo enables the
reader to sense grace at work, hinted at in the concluding
lines quoted above. It's not an intellectually solid theodicy,
but it describes a lived truth: even the most faithful believer
questions God in the face of suffering. If he or she doesn't,
they are surely lacking in humanity. Endo shows us that
there is grace in this struggle, that the struggle with faith in
suffering has a purpose. Even as Rodrigues is overwhelmed,
he gives absolution to the treacherous Kichijiro. There is
something here of grace at work even in dis-grace, an echo
of St Paul's frequent references to his weakness: 'When I
am weak then I am strong' (2 Cor. 12:10).

It's easy to think that grace is a gift given to those whose
prayer or moral conduct has earned it. Endo describes
the disturbing fact that grace is always unmerited, pure
gift. We cannot demand it, we can only long for it; we
long to know that our life has meaning, even as we fear
that our life is a dis-grace. *Silence* is a story where the
grace is in the longing.

LISTENING TO SILENCE: CONTEMPLATION

Endo shows rather than explains that the language
of grace includes both words and silence in the same
way that conversation does. To practise silence is in
many ways to practise longing for the God who is

silent. Or to put it another way, when I am silent then perhaps I can hear something of God's silence. And God's silence contains a meaning, like the love of two people who can sit together without saying a word and be happy in each other's company. Silent contemplation is a mirror of God, a mirror of grace at work in the soul.

It comes as a surprise when we realize that silence is an essential part of language. Silence is needed to break up sounds to form discrete words, and it's needed as part of a conversation. The ability to stay silent and really listen requires an effort. It's sometimes more natural for people just to chatter, and in some situations that's fine; a supermarket checkout queue is a place for friendly but predictable remarks like 'How are you' and 'Not so bad' rather than careful listening. But in other contexts, careful listening is an act of kindness.

An ancient story illustrates this. It's told by one of the first Christian monks and nuns who lived in the Middle East during the fourth and fifth centuries, known collectively as the Desert Fathers and Mothers.

There were three earnest men who were friends and became monks. One chose to live out the saying 'Blessed are the peacemakers', and worked to reconcile enemies. The second chose to visit the sick. But the third went to live in the desert and stayed in solitude. Now the first worked among many contentious people and found that he could not appease them all, so eventually he was overcome with exhaustion. He sought out his friend who was caring for the sick, only to find that he too was worn out, depressed and unable to carry on. The two of them decided to visit their friend who lived in the desert, and they told him all their troubles. When they asked him how he was, the monk was silent for a while and then poured some water into a bowl. 'Look at the water,' he said, and they saw that it was murky. After a while he said, 'Look again and see how clear the water has become.' As they looked, the two monks saw their own faces as in a mirror. And the monk said to his friends: 'Because of the turbulence of life, the one who lives amid activity does not see his sins. But when he is quiet, especially in solitude, then he sees the real state of things.'

This does not mean that aiming to serve others and work hard is bad. It is a question of balance. In the monastic tradition, silent solitude is seen as a necessary part of life, not an optional extra. To know yourself and to grow require the insights that only solitude can provide. Even the most intimate friendship is no substitute for the work that we must do on our own, the work of silent reflection and prayer. Contemplation is a key element of the language of grace.

A consideration of silence in daily life is a good place to start thinking about how to practise silence. In my experience, people who come on retreat for the first time find it hard to spend some time in silence, even though at one level this is what they crave and why they have come. They are often shocked to discover that, no sooner have they removed the daily routine, set aside the TV and found a place of silence, than their head fills up with trivial thoughts. 'I wonder what's for supper? I need to book an appointment with the dentist. I need to write to my cousin ...' To their shame and embarrassment people discover that the busy-ness of life has got right inside their heads and they can't get it out. To empty their heads of all thoughts, words and images is almost impossible, yet somehow these distressing internal noises need to be calmed down. Perseverance is needed to clear one's head not only in order to be silent with God, but also in order to be silent in conversation with others.

LISTENING TO WORDS: DISCERNMENT

To be good at conversation, we need to learn when to be silent and listen, and when to speak. When another person is speaking, I can choose to focus on what I'm going to say next, in which case I'm only half listening. By contrast, I can choose to set aside my own thoughts and listen deeply to the other person. A deep listener lets the other person finish, may pause before responding, and then says something that connects thoughtfully with what's just been said. If the other person needs comfort or support, it's often enough simply to reflect back what's just been said to show it's been understood. 'Thank you for listening' is a regular response to such a conversation. All too often, however, people want to say something like, 'I know how you feel' (which is by definition untrue) or, 'Well, you've still got such-and-such' (which ignores the distress at what's been lost). The skill of silent listening is of great value to both the listener and the speaker. To feel understood by someone is to feel they are trustworthy; to be quiet and listen carefully to another person's words is to build trust. Silence is part of the language of grace.

There are two saints renowned for their skill in listening: the Italian Benedict of Nursia born in 480, and the Basque Ignatius of Loyola, born a thousand years later. Both are Catholic saints and authors of guides to living in a religious community.

The opening word of the Rule of St Benedict is 'listen' – but listen to what? 'Listen to the master's instructions.' Listen how? 'Attend with the ear of your heart.' The ear of the heart is a challenging phrase for modern readers of the Rule, but it is an important metaphor for the kind of spiritual listening needed when listening out for words of grace. To understand this very particular skill, it will help to consider how people listen to spoken words in general.

In simple terms, the human ear hears words and the brain then processes the sounds to generate the meaning of those words. But it's not the words alone that convey the meaning of a sentence. In *How Language Works* Professor David Crystal gives an example of how intonation and pause (shown here in the punctuation) can change the meaning of the same words. Consider 'She dressed, and fed the baby' (i.e. the person dressed herself, and then fed the baby) versus 'She dressed and fed the baby' (i.e. the baby is both dressed and fed). These intonations and pauses are also heard by the human ear, but they are not processed by the brain into different meanings until the hearer is nearly adult. Crystal refers to research which shows how distinguishing these subtle aural clues is a skill not usually acquired until the late teenage years. This is the climax of a long process of language learning that begins at birth. Within a few days of birth, babies turn their heads when their mothers speak; they understand a few words by the end of their first year, and can say some words at age two. Learning to interpret the subtleties of pauses and intonations, however, takes another 16 or so years. Listening to speech, therefore, is not just one activity but involves many different layers of activity, and takes many years to perfect.

The listening activity indicated by the term 'ear of the heart' is acquired even later in life and requires careful schooling. That's why St Benedict wants to set up what he calls 'a school of the Lord's service'. A key skill for the leader of this school, the abbot, is that he must be 'discerning' and show 'discretion, the mother of the virtues' so that his decisions are wise. For Benedict, to discern with discretion is to make choices that help in the development of a truly spiritual life. The monastery provides a rhythm of life and learning to help people become skilled at making those choices. A crucial choice is whether somebody should be allowed to join the monastery in the first place. Novices, he says, are not to be admitted easily because, quoting scripture, Benedict wants to 'test the spirits to see if they come from God' (1 Jn 4.1).

There are good spirits and there are bad spirits, and distinguishing between the two requires discernment. While people today might not use those exact words, similar terms are still used: somebody can be called 'mean-spirited', an action is done in 'a generous spirit', a musician can give 'a spirited performance'. In some situations, people know instinctively if there is a good or a bad spirit present. This distinction can also be made at a deeper level in a person's inner world of thoughts and feelings. We all have good and bad spirits inside us, but they are not always easy for an individual to distinguish without the help of another person. This testing of the spirits is a key task of the spiritual listening known as discernment, and it is taken to a new level by St Ignatius.

While those who follow the Rule of Benedict live in monasteries, Ignatius started a whole new way of belonging to a religious order. His brothers would live a way of life very different from monks. They would not wear habits or live around cloisters behind walls, celebrating offices in Church and doing manual labour. Instead, his band of brothers would be modelled on an army and would go out into the whole world to fight for the Catholic Faith, armed not with weapons but with charity, prayer and a practical spirituality rooted in the discernment of spirits. Ignatius himself was inspired to this way of life during a stay at the Benedictine abbey of Montserrat near Barcelona. He learned there about the discernment of spirits, but then built that skill into a whole new approach to spirituality, his Spiritual Exercises. The community he founded is called the Society of Jesus, known as the Jesuits, and the heroes of *Silence* are all priests of that society.

In an interview, the current Father General of the Society of Jesus, Father Sosa, has described what happened to St Ignatius as follows: 'St Ignatius experienced a great transformation when he learned to read his own feelings and to find in his own experience how God was guiding him.' A monk at Montserrat who listened to him over many weeks helped him to sense the movement of the spirits in his own life and to test them. He used his imagination to relive the life of Christ in his mind's eye so that it might become the template for distinguishing good spirits from bad spirits. He became attentive to some repeated patterns – for example, the bad spirit dressed as an angel of light – and how to see through that deception. 'Discernment', says Fr Sosa, 'is to learn to go behind what appears, beyond what rationality can teach you, beyond normal knowledge, to be open to the signs of the Spirit in life, your own life and the life of others.' All this and more St Ignatius built into the Spiritual Exercises, a 30-day silent retreat during which a person is accompanied by a spiritual director for one hour a day. A Jesuit must follow the Exercises once in his first year as a novice and again at the end of his formation. 'The purpose of the Spiritual Exercises', Fr Sosa continues, 'is to search and to find. Election (choice) is the proof of spiritual discernment. You need to make a decision, to find God's will.' Ignatius knew, however, that, to make a good decision, the one making the decision had to be in a state of what he called consolation; the opposite of this is desolation, or what might nowadays be called depression, not necessarily clinical depression but a lack of awareness of the goodness of life and the love of God. To decide well a person needs to be in a state of gratitude.

This intense training is not only the foundation of the Jesuit's own life, but it also enables him to guide others in their discernment. The role of the spiritual director is central to the Exercises, and the text Ignatius wrote describing them is for the director. The director must be an attentive listener, listening not only to the words but to the hidden depths within and around them. This parallels the recognition of meaning in the intonations and pauses of language described earlier. Spiritual direction involves listening to the language of grace as it emerges from within somebody's description of their experience. This involves listening to what's said and then nudging the person to say more about certain aspects of what they describe. And of what they do not describe. The director is listening out for grace at work in the person's life, grace of which that person may not be aware and which the director helps them to explore.

My own experience of this kind of listening (both as a listener and a speaker) is that the listener receives a word or phrase from the speaker and holds onto it for a moment, holding it in front of the speaker, inviting them to explore it. The skill of the listener is knowing which words to let pass and which to catch.

The possibility of both doing and leading the Spiritual Exercises is now offered to members of other religious orders, to ministers of other denominations and to lay people. One of the most remarkable examples of the effects of this wider availability of the Exercises is seen in the Swedish prison system.

Truls Bernhold, a Lutheran minister, completed the Exercises in England in 2000, and in 2001 he was invited to lead a meditation group in Kumla Prison, the largest in Sweden, that houses the country's highest-risk prisoners. The effect of the meditation course on the prisoners involved impressed the authorities. A disused building was therefore converted to accommodate eight prisoners in a retreat centre known as 'the monastery'. There Truls began to lead prisoners in a 30-day retreat using the Spiritual Exercises of St Ignatius. He listened to the prisoner and invited him to meditate on a passage of the Gospel. The prisoner then read that passage, listened to his own reaction to it and shared that with Truls at the next session. This basic pattern was then repeated over the 30 days with an emphasis on different aspects of the prisoner's life and different episodes in the life of Christ. There are many examples of prisoners' lives transformed at Kumla by the careful listening of a spiritual director guiding them through the Spiritual Exercises. The Swedish Prison Service said this was their most effective rehabilitation programme.

I visited the Kumla monastery in 2013 and met the minister who took over from Truls in 2008 and ran the full retreat twice a year. She explained that any prisoner in the Swedish prison system could apply to do the Exercises at Kumla, and that they had more requests than places. Consequently, after selection, prisoners do a one-week retreat to see if they are suitable for the full 30 days.

I was introduced to Carlos (not his real name), a man in his twenties serving a very long sentence that suggested he was in prison for a serious and violent crime (long prison sentences are rare in Sweden). When he entered the prison, he explained to me, he was filled with rage and wouldn't speak to anybody, not even fellow prisoners. He loathed the warders and applied to do the retreat merely to get away from other people.

During his initial daily meetings with the retreat director he gave monosyllabic answers, but gradually he spoke more, so the director helped him to name his rage and slowly move beyond it. Those 30 days changed his life, Carlos told me, and now he was one of those who helped with the running of the retreats. I saw him embrace a warder who came into the monastery. 'He's my friend!' he explained, and the warder returned the gesture warmly.

It's striking that the prisoners who participate are not necessarily converted to Christian faith. Carlos reconnected with the Catholic faith of his Latino upbringing, but some discover other paths. Meditating on the life of Christ is central to the Exercises, but that doesn't necessarily lead to an explicitly religious conversion or initiation into a faith community.

In 2019, the Swedish prison service experienced a shortage of prison cells, having previously closed prisons because of falling numbers. At short notice, prisons were required to make ancillary spaces available to house prisoners. To the dismay of the Kumla prison authorities, the monastery wing was turned into cells for prisoners and the project closed. For 18 years, however, this project not only helped transform prisoners' lives but also was a living example of how the language of grace works: listening to what is said by the prisoner and finding there traces of grace to build upon; then offering episodes from the life of Christ for the prisoner to reflect upon, and listening again to how he responds to them; leading to a choice by the prisoner about how he will live in future. At its heart, this is about listening to the language of grace forming on the lips of the prisoner and encouraging him to stay with that language and the insights it brings, then offering sacred texts to feed those insights. The retreat leader does not proselytize: she lets grace do its work.

The work of the Kumla monastery opens up the scope of how grace works beyond the boundaries of formal religious categories. There is a fine explanation of this from the man who would become Pope Benedict XVI. In 1969, Joseph Ratzinger wrote about 'the dissemination of scripture among non-Christians'. He noted that the Catholic Church's mission 'had hitherto been too hierarchically and institutionally-minded', and urged the Church to have 'confidence in the self-active power of the word ... far beyond the area of the hierarchical Church'. By simply offering people the words of scripture, he went on, the presence of Christ 'is made possible in this way among the unbaptised and those who will largely remain unbaptised'. Ratzinger concludes with a reference to the story of a sick woman who didn't meet Christ but who sought healing by reaching out from the crowd to touch his clothes as he walked along. 'What it means when men and women are perhaps only able to touch, as it were, the fringe of the garment of the Lord as he passes by, ultimately only he himself can know.' This sums up beautifully the work of the Kumla monastery.

People sometimes say 'so-and-so needs a good talking to,' but there is the alternative possibility that somebody might need a good listening to. If we are listened to well there is a chance that we will in turn become good at listening to others, including the divine other. Listening and being listened to are vital parts of the language of grace.

LISTENING EXERCISES

Listening to other people
Choose a couple of days (preferably not too busy) when you will consciously develop your awareness of how you react during conversations. Notice the following:

1 When you're listening to another person speak, what else are you thinking about?
2 How might you become better at listening more attentively to what the other person is saying?
3 Can you hear something 'behind' or 'around' what another person is saying?

Could you describe some of this as the good spirit and some as the bad spirit?

Relating to other people
Recall a relationship that you find difficult. What sort of misunderstandings occur in this relationship? How might listening more carefully reduce misunderstandings?

Spiritual direction
Consider asking for a spiritual director from the Mount St Jesuit Centre, London or other spirituality centre.

Speaking

*May the spoken words of my mouth ... win favour
in your sight, O Lord.*

Psalm 19

THE LEGEND OF NOT SPEAKING

There can be grace in speaking and there can be grace
in silence. Knowing when to speak and when to remain
silent is the key skill to be explored in this chapter; that
skill is in itself a grace. St Benedict calls his chapter
on silence 'On Being Taciturn', which means 'on
restraining the urge to speak'. He begins with the words
of the psalm: 'I have resolved to keep watch over my
ways so that I may not sin with my tongue.' The tongue
as a source of evil is something our very communicative
era does not consider very often. We think that 'saying
what is on your mind' is a good thing; Benedict is not so
sure. He quotes the Book of Proverbs twice: 'In a flood
of words you will not avoid sin' (Prov. 10.19) and 'The
tongue holds the key to life and death' (Prov. 18.21).

Vulgarity and gossip are particularly frowned upon, especially if they lead to laughter. Benedict prohibits all the talk we indulge in 'just for a laugh'.

More positively, St Paul says: 'Your speech should always be gracious, flavoured with wit [literally 'with salt']' (Col. 4.6). What unites the Benedictine and the Pauline attitude to speech, however, is that speech should be an intentional act, something undertaken thoughtfully, and not just mindless chatter. One of those quotations from Proverbs puts this very starkly: speech is a matter of life and death. One of the great European legends illustrates this powerfully: the legend of Perceval and the Holy Grail.

The earliest version of this legend was written in the twelfth century by the French poet Chrétien de Troyes. He wrote several romances that featured the legendary King Arthur, the fifth-century Romano-Briton who, after the departure of the Romans, defended the country against the invading Anglo-Saxons. Within this legendary world, the Welsh are simple, rural people, unaffected by Roman culture, living amid mists and mountains. For the dominant French culture of twelfth-century England, the Welsh were an inferior race, and yet the hero of the Grail legend from a Frenchman's pen is the Welsh youth, Perceval.

Like Endo's Jesuit priests, Perceval was on a journey, but where Fr Rodrigues was defeated by God's silence, Perceval was wounded by his own silence. At a critical point in the journey, he failed to say the right thing, with terrible consequences.

The story begins with a nameless teenage boy living with his widowed mother on a farm in the Waste Forest.

It is 'the season when trees flower, shrubs leaf, meadows grow green and birds in their own tongue sing sweetly in the mornings'. The boy saddles up his hunter to go and see some workers nearby. On his way, he encounters five armed knights, and is 'captivated and astonished' by the sight of them, because he has never seen or heard of knights. The leading knight asks the boy for information about some travellers, but the boy repeatedly ignores the question; in turn he asks the knight, 'What is this?' about every item of his knightly equipment. While the birds have 'their own tongue', the future hero has no language with which to name what he sees, and ignores what the knight is asking. He is tongue-tied and deaf to what was said. 'Sir', one of the other knights concludes, 'you must be aware that all Welshmen are by nature more stupid than the beasts in the fields.'

Perceval lacks the language of knighthood, yet instantly wants to be a knight. On returning to his mother, she reveals that his father and two brothers were knights who died when he was an infant, the brothers in combat and the father from grief. She begs him not to follow their example.

'I don't understand your words,' says the boy to his mother, 'but I would gladly go to the king who makes knights; and I will go no matter what.' Now, not only does he not understand the knights, but he also doesn't understand his mother. He is a language orphan. At every stage of the legend, the inability to grasp or say appropriate words is pivotal. Perceval sets out to find King Arthur, in one sense to find a new language. He finds the King, kills a knight and acquires his magnificent armour, but still has no idea how to use knightly weapons. He has the kit but not the skill, a kid with the latest technology and no idea how to use it.

After numerous adventures, the story takes a new turn. On his journey home, Perceval's way is blocked by a river with no means of crossing it on horseback. A man fishing from a boat tells him where to find lodging and, on the way, a magnificent castle suddenly appears. There, the young knight is greeted warmly and invited to sit next to a disabled but noble lord in a vast hall. Before they eat, a silent procession of a most unusual kind passes before them. Among the items in the procession are a lance tipped with blood and a golden, jewel-encrusted grail or cup accompanied by servants holding candelabra. 'The young knight watched them pass by but did not dare ask who was served from the grail ... at times it is just as wrong to keep too silent as to talk too much.' While he can't stop asking questions about the knight's equipment, faced by these spiritual objects he is dumbfounded.

Without realizing it, the young knight has entered the Grail Castle. He has seen the lance that pierced Christ's side on the cross and the cup used at the Last Supper. He has entered a transcendent world and encountered divine life – but he has no idea what is happening and no language with which to enquire.

The next day, the hapless youth meets a young lady who explains that the lord of the castle was the Fisher King, wounded in his thighs, who only found solace in a fishing boat. The lady turns out to be his cousin, and reveals that his name is Perceval. She is anxious to know if he asked about the items in the mysterious procession. 'No question came from my mouth,' he replies. His cousin is distraught:

> How unfortunate you were when you failed to ask all this, because you would have brought great succour to the king who is maimed; he would have totally regained the use of his limbs and ruled his lands, and much good would have come of it. But understand this now: much suffering will befall you and others.

Perceval's life then goes downhill and he gradually loses his mind. After numerous incidents, the narrator tells us that 'Perceval ... had lost his memory so totally that he no longer remembered God.' For five years, he never enters a church, but finally, one Good Friday, he meets a hermit who identifies the source of his decline: 'When you did not enquire who is served from the grail, you committed folly.' Perceval does penance until Easter Sunday, when he 'very worthily received communion'. At this point, Chrétien's story of Perceval ends abruptly, though other medieval authors wrote several continuations.

FINDING YOUR VOICE

The therapist and theologian Professor Peter Tyler sees in the Perceval legend a fundamental human experience.

> When the inevitable encounter with the transcendent does occur – and occur it

must – many young people today will have
no conceptual framework with which to make
sense of it. It may appear weird, an irrelevance,
or indeed a mental pathology or psychosis. Like
Perceval, they will stumble into the Grail Castle
totally unprepared.

The legend illustrates how speaking the language of
grace is a vital life skill. Without it kings lie wounded,
knights lose their memory and a whole country suffers.
'Who is served from the grail?' was the question not
asked, the question that could have been the gateway
to universal healing. At the end of the story, the grail
is revealed to be the vessel from which the Fisher King
receives a consecrated host once a day as his sole food.
Here is the answer to the unasked question: this is the
vessel through which Christ serves the wounded king.
The wounded king is so holy that he lives on the Body
of Christ as his sole food. In addition to universal
healing, the answer to the right question couched in
the right language would have guided Perceval into
many dimensions of grace: a deeper relationship with
the Fisher King, an encounter with the transcendent
and a realization that he was in the presence of God.

There's an important contrast between the questions
Perceval asked the knight and the question he didn't
ask about the grail. He repeatedly asked the about the
knight's equipment: 'What's this and what is it used
for?', a very functional question. Whereas 'Who is
served from the grail?' is a personal question about
attending to another's needs: who does the grail serve?

Even though this is a story about the fifth century written in the twelfth century, its contemporary themes are striking: a fatherless adolescent boy who leaves home against his mother's will; his fascination with 'stuff' and a headlong rush to seek all that 'stuff' offers; his lack of spiritual vocabulary that leads him to botch a profound spiritual experience, failing to ask the right question; growing despair and loss of identity leading not simply to loss of faith in God but to forgetting about God completely. This is a pattern familiar to those who work with the young today. If the young person finds their hermit, redemption follows, but in the UK the last ten years have seen cuts to local youth services and a rise in teenage mental health problems. There are too few adults willing and able to mentor those who've lost their way and their identity.

This mentoring is not simply telling somebody what to do; rather it's coaching young people to find their own voice, so that they can ask the right question about who they will serve and how they can perform that service. In so far as it involves teaching, it's teaching them to speak authentically. For many, a good school and a good local community provide the mentors and role models who can supply this 'voice coaching'. For others, however, daring new approaches are needed to provide such mentoring.

One such new approach is Courtyard, a project run by a Catholic youth charity to train parishes in offering support to young people on the margins of the local community, irrespective of their faith background. Many adults are aware of young people hanging out in groups not doing much but creating a rather menacing atmosphere. This project supports parishes to engage with these young people in a way that is measured and safe, leading to an invitation to a 'courtyard' set aside for their use. Such detached youth work, as it's called, is not an invitation to a youth club. It is an encounter on the street that might lead to some young people expressing their aspirations in a space provided for them, with the support of older people. This is a courtyard for asking and answering the right questions.

I helped in a small way to set up the pilot parishes of this project, and saw parishioners learn from trained youth workers how to walk their own neighbourhood in twos and threes. From one parish I heard how they observed where the young gathered and what was distinctive about each group. Repeating the walk at the same time each week, they identified that often there were core members and then there were hangers-on. After some weeks, they risked smiling at the hangers-on of one group. If the smile was reciprocated, they risked a 'hi', and in time one or two peeled away to follow them to ask who they were. From this dialogue came an invitation to visit the parish hall and use it one night a week as their courtyard for whatever activity they chose. The young people were dumbfounded; nobody had ever offered them such a facility and such an opportunity, with no strings attached. They chose to get involved in the parish talent show, creating videos to advertise the project, and several of the young people left the street corner to give expression to their voices on stage.

The rise of youth-on-youth knife crime had a significant impact on this project, especially when a friend of the group was murdered on a nearby street. The trauma of this event made the volunteers fearful and start to lose confidence at just the time when the project was most needed. The future remains uncertain and so, as with the Perceval legend, this story has a redeeming climax but an abrupt and ambiguous ending that others may continue elsewhere.

SPEAKING WITH PEOPLE ALONG THE ROAD

The gospel story of the disciples on the road to Emmaus describes a stranger approaching people on the street and helping them find their voice. Two disheartened men are walking away from Jerusalem, leaving behind their community, whose leader has just been executed. A stranger joins them on the road and hears how their hopes have been dashed by this turn of events. The stranger then gives them an alternative interpretation of those events, mentioning some bible texts; what he says encourages them, so that evening they invite him to stay and eat with them. The stranger says grace and then shares out the bread, at which point they realize that the stranger is Jesus, who immediately vanishes. What confirms that this was indeed Jesus was the way he spoke to them: 'Were not our hearts burning within us as he talked to us on the road?' Gracious speaking is a hallmark of Jesus, as it is for many good people, but his language of grace is also a way of life.

This way of grace involves listening before speaking, even when someone is getting things wrong and heading in the wrong direction. Jesus stays with the disciples even as they make the mistake of walking away from Jerusalem. After Jesus speaks to them and after the revelation at the breaking of bread, they turn round and head back to Jerusalem, where they belong. The way he speaks touches their hearts and enables them to turn their lives around without his telling them.

Original mistrust means that it's hard to give somebody the space to figure things out for themselves. How can they be trusted to do this? Surely somebody should just tell them what's best? In some circumstances, there are times when a straight order is the right approach; for example, when somebody is about to do something that will harm others it's OK to say 'Stop!' Similarly when putting in place regulations about safety, the rules of a game or the conventions of a process. But in personal decision-making, the helpful speaking of a good accompanier can release the hearer's voice. The accompanier must make the intentional choice to trust the hearer. The person accompanied can then find the confidence to trust their own judgement; they 'catch' trust from the other person and have the confidence to choose their own future. They will not always choose what the accompanier thinks is best, but they will own the consequences.

I've had the privilege of being invited by young people to accompany them as they seek to discern their vocation. This rarely goes the way I think it will go, but it always teaches me to be patient. I listen for words that are a cue for me to speak, rather than just waiting for the other person to stop speaking so I can offer my opinion. This is the difference between a discernment conversation and a debate. My conviction in faith is that, in a discernment conversation, both of us are listening out for the Holy Spirit, for the movements of the human spirit where the Holy Spirit is active. My challenge to myself is to speak only those words that can help that discovery process. For example, maybe I'm in conversation with a young man who has wanted to be a priest all his life and who I think is a good potential candidate. During the discernment conversations, he gradually realizes that this conviction is his own idea and is blocking the work of the Spirit in his life; I resist the urge to recruit him for the seminary. Or I may be talking to a person who is convinced she must leave her employment in a bank and become a teacher; at first, this seems laudable, but I must set aside that thought and respond to what she says. Gradually, through our conversations and to my surprise, she realizes that the bank is not the problem, she is.

This kind of accompaniment can happen in many contexts: the formal conversations I've just described; a conversation between friends; a conversation during a pilgrimage; a conversation with a teacher or mentor. The key to this way of grace is good speaking and good listening on both sides.

In such conversations, whether on the road to Emmaus or any road, the language of grace is powerfully at work, channelling grace, inviting grace, seeking grace. This is grace that changes people for the better and helps them take personal responsibility for their lives. Some people come to this conversational grace easily, others will only turn to it when they've lived through a period of self-destructive behaviour, and others still will never discover its joy, because their original mistrust of others overwhelms their capacity to speak and listen graciously.

JESUS THE STORYTELLER

So far in this chapter we've looked at two stories: a medieval legend and part of a Gospel. Both show great storytelling skills on the part of the author. One of the reasons the Gospels are such enduring texts is that they are well written and we'll be looking at writing as a spiritual activity later. For now, let's look at another literary feature of the Gospels, Jesus's skill as a storyteller. This is no accidental feature of his life and ministry. Jesus does not speak in riddles, using brain teasers or puzzles like a murder mystery author. While rabbis to this day tell parables, the stories Jesus tells are like his healings: they not only describe grace (usually calling it the Kingdom of God), they also perform what they describe. People and culture are changed by the stories Jesus tells.

From Luke's Gospel comes the parable of the Good Samaritan. When some years ago I read this to a well-educated young woman her response was, 'I always wondered where that expression came from.' Like most of her generation, she had little or no knowledge of the Bible, but the phrase 'a good Samaritan' is still part of contemporary culture and carries a strong, positive meaning.

This illustrates an important aspect of Jesus's storytelling. His stories are not simply similes or metaphors, even though Matthew's Gospel often introduces them by saying 'the kingdom of heaven is like ...' Luke's Gospel simply says 'he told them this parable.' Both writers make it clear, however, that the parables are not simply moral lessons: they are establishing the kingdom of

God. The kingdom of God is the grace of God at work in this world, not in a particular country but in people's lives, ultimately revealed in the life to come. Parables are Jesus's way of making grace recognizable, felt and accepted. The reason Jesus speaks in parables is not clear to his disciples, however, and three of the Gospels describe them asking for an explanation. 'The reason I talk to them in parables', says Jesus in Matthew's Gospel, 'is that they look without seeing and listen without hearing or understanding.'

Let's unpack this cryptic sentence by looking at the reason why Jesus told the parable of the Good Samaritan. A lawyer was testing him, the text says, and had just heard Jesus say love your neighbour as yourself, so he asked, 'And who is my neighbour?' Jesus could have replied: anybody who is in distress. That's the moral message of the parable, so why did Jesus tell the whole parable? The story itself answers that question. It involves three characters who came across a wounded traveller on the roadside. Two of them 'passed by on the other side'. The third, a Samaritan, was 'moved with compassion when he saw him' and carried him to the safety of an inn. Jesus does not end there: he poses a question back to the lawyer: 'Who proved himself a neighbour to the man?' And the lawyer has to answer: 'The one who showed mercy towards him.' 'Go and do the same,' is Jesus's final word.

Having told the parable, Jesus could then invert the original question and challenge the lawyer at a personal level. In this way, the lawyer, a Jewish expert on the law of Moses, is drawn into a story that challenges

his whole world. First, he is forced to admit that a
Jewish priest and a Levite behaved badly, and secondly
he has to name a Samaritan, an enemy of the people
of Israel, as the good guy. Having turned the tables
on the lawyer, Jesus then challenges him to change
the way he lives. By means of the parable, Jesus's
answer is transformed into a personal challenge to the
questioner. Jesus takes the original question 'Who is
my neighbour?' and turns it round to become 'Who
proved himself neighbour to the man?' The lawyer is
invited to make a choice about who showed himself
to be a neighbour in the story, and to live out the
implications of that choice.

The story of the Good Samaritan shows how a
parable is not simply a story that carries a message. If
it was merely that, then people could 'listen without
hearing or understanding'; in other words, ignore it.
Frankly, 'be nice to people in distress' is easy advice
to ignore. By contrast, the parables of Jesus have
this existential bite to them which means any honest
listener *must* respond; all credit to the lawyer that he
did listen and respond without shying away. When
someone responds positively to a parable, grace flows
through their life. In that way, a parable is a story
that performs what it describes; that's why Jesus uses
parables. His mission was to proclaim the coming of
the kingdom of grace, and the parables make that
kingdom a reality.

I intentionally use the present tense in the final phrase
of that last sentence: parables still make grace a reality.
The Jewish gift for storytelling is a gift to the whole world,

and the parables of Jesus are part of that great legacy. Yet to retell one of those parables is also once again to bring about the kingdom of grace, provided we wish to do good by telling it. Each time the story is read aloud or in private, the listener or reader is challenged to be a neighbour to those wounded at the side of their road.

During the pandemic lockdown, people have been challenged to choose the people to whom they will be a neighbour: shopping for people who were shielding, keeping in touch with young people suffering mentally, looking out for friends and relations via phone calls or knocks on the door. More broadly, seeking to build back better by making communities more neighbourly to the weakest. The story of the wounded traveller invites us to make choices, an invitation given new urgency by the pandemic.

The echo of that first telling of the parable of the Good Samaritan still resounds through the world, not only inspiring those who hear it but also describing humanity at its best among those who have never heard it. This is gracious speaking of the highest order.

SPEAKING WELL TODAY

So how can people learn to speak like Jesus? If the language of grace makes grace a reality as in the parables of Jesus, how can we learn to speak it? That is not simply a pious question. It's also a psycho-linguistic question: is there a psychology of gracious speaking? Psychologists can help people overcome certain fears and phobias, so can psychologists and language experts help people to speak graciously? Why does a person speak or not speak? To return to where this chapter began, why couldn't Perceval speak at the vital moment? These are challenging questions, because the answers are not as clear cut as the resounding yes that can be given to teaching people to listen well, to write well and to read well. Reading and writing are taught in every school curriculum, while listening well is one of a person's earliest skills, as Professor David Crystal reminds us. Experiments have shown that day-old babies attend to their mother's voice but not to strangers, and that within two weeks they prefer human voices to other sounds. 'Abilities of this kind are so apparent,' he concludes, 'that some auditory training must begin within the womb.' By contrast, he baldly states, 'Children learning the sounds of speech have quite a mountain to climb.' I think people also have a mountain to climb when it comes to learning the sounds of gracious speech.

Without intentional training, original mistrust can dominate the way we speak. It's easy to adopt an aggressive and an unforgiving tone as a standard way of speaking, especially if we feel insecure or vulnerable. In the case of people bullied and mistreated by others, this is not surprising; they give as good as they get. In the school playground, this can sometimes be a workable strategy: stick up for yourself and the others will respect you. Beyond the world of the playground, however, a more gracious approach can pay dividends.

I listened in awe as one survivor of childhood sexual abuse, decades after he had been abused by a priest, described asking to meet his abuser so that he could forgive him. He wanted to do this not for the sake of the abuser but for his own sake, as a way of letting go of the past and moving forwards. Speaking words of forgiveness in those circumstances requires a rare degree of self-possession and self-confidence: the very qualities that abuse takes away.

Just as difficult is the situation of a person whose loved ones and even their own limbs are taken away by accident. This can lead to rage against life and against God. The British Paralympian Stef Reid MBE was a keen teenage athlete, but at the age of 16 lost a foot in a boating accident. Speaking to young people before the London Paralympics 2012, she described how devastated she was that all her hopes for a sporting life had gone.

> But I gave God the benefit of the doubt, and through my grief and devastation I trusted him. But it was confusing. Why should God bless me with passion and ability for sport only to take it away? How was I going to be me? Would I still enjoy life? Over the next few months and years, God revealed to me that he put my drive and love for competition in me for a reason. I didn't need to change: I just needed to apply it in a different way.

Stef had already won Paralympic bronze in 2008 as a sprinter. 'Twelve years ago', she concluded, 'lying in my hospital bed, short of one foot, being a professional runner was the last thing I expected of my life. But we serve a mighty God!' She went on to win silver for the long jump in the 2012 Paralympics. Her life is a story of rage that led on to grace, and her talk to 10,000 young people at Wembley Arena was an example of speaking the language of grace entirely naturally. She had landed on her one foot, and was so grounded in grace that it flowed through her words to the audience.

Away from such traumatic situations, people can learn to speak graciously day to day. Before the pandemic lockdown, I had noticed during my own travels over the years a considerable increase in the abusive language directed towards staff on public transport. People seemed to give themselves the right to swear at staff and to demean them. My awareness of this increased verbal violence as a widespread phenomenon was sharpened when, for the first time, signs were posted at railway stations stating that staff had a right to work in a safe environment and that aggressive behaviour would be reported to the police. During the pandemic lockdown, public transport staff continued to work, some losing their lives to the disease. As the restrictions eased, I ventured out and noticed lots of people thanking bus drivers as they disembarked. Thankfulness for bin men also became a theme of conversation. Alongside the 'clap for carers', I think there is and will be greater appreciation of those who work in the public sector, often on low pay. Expressing gratitude for public sector workers is gracious speaking.

It's the intentionality of these gracious ways of speaking that strikes me: the intention to forgive, the intention to thank. The only way our speech can avoid expressing mistrust and aggression is if we consciously train ourselves to speak well. That's what St Benedict means when he reflects 'on being taciturn': when you do speak, make sure it's something worth saying, that brings light, not darkness.

Connected to this is how we deal with anger. 'It's good to let off steam' is something people say to justify expressing anger, but this implies that a human being is like a steam engine. In a way, losing your temper is just that; tempered steel is stronger than ordinary steel, so to lose your temper is to diminish your humanity. Loss of temper happens, but it's not good for you, and can damage the speaker as well as the hearer. Cognitive behaviour therapy offers skills to control anger and to reframe it into a different emotion such as compassion for the person provoking your anger.

Intentionally choosing to step away from rage is a learnt skill that protects everybody concerned. Much anger is provoked by personal slights that wound our pride; if we can see that, then we can choose to embrace humility and ignore it. This also gives us the inner freedom to express moral indignation when we see real injustice done to others or to ourselves. Speaking out against wrongdoing shows passion for justice and can be another form of gracious speaking, but it is distinct from the anger that comes from wounded pride. The ability to distinguish the two requires a high level of self-awareness.

This thoughtful approach to language is thankfully still strong in daily life in families: 'Don't speak to your mother like that,' a father might say to a bolshy child. And a recent survey by the British Board of Film Classification found that, even though the number of people who admitted to strong swearing had increased by a third in five years, 75 per cent of parents still don't like their children swearing, and would avoid swearing if somebody under 16 is present. People seem to know instinctively that gracious speaking is the better way, but they need help to learn how to sustain the language of grace day by day.

SPEAKING EXERCISES

Keep a language diary with headings such as:

People I thanked today/people I should have thanked
Occasions I expressed anger/occasions I should
    have expressed outrage but kept quiet
Times I asked a good question/times I failed to ask
    the right question

That last one could be called the Perceval category.

In the diary, keep a list of the main topics of conversation that day apart from work topics, giving lengths of time if possible. At the end of the week, discover what you spent most time speaking about.

Ask somebody you trust to have a conversation about how you come across to other people in the way you speak. You may have to press them to say more than 'You sound fine.'

Taken together, these exercises add up to an informal inventory of your way of speaking, and can form the basis for intentionally choosing the language of grace.

4

Writing

Thus says the Lord, the God of Israel, 'Write all the words which I have spoken to you in a book.'

Ep. Jr 30.2

WHAT IS WRITING?

Writing is the only form of language that by its very nature endures. Speech and reading out loud only survive by means of electronic reproduction, while listening and reading to oneself have no permanent expression. As the ancient Romans put it: words fly away, writing remains.

Ewan Clayton, the calligrapher and author of *The Golden Thread: The Story of Writing*, explains how writing works.

> We identify it, quite obviously, with the
> visible things, the tools, the materials, the marks
> on the paper or whatever. But what writing really
> is at a deeper level is a social phenomenon, it's

a social technology. It's made up of agreements
around certain shapes that they stand for
something.

These 'agreements' are often challenged by those who
write the language of grace. Writers of grace break the
bounds of conventional language as they describe the
divine love hidden within daily life. A particular feature
of such writing is that the words transcend divisions and
mistrust, often portraying grace in the midst of conflict.
Current writing trends push language in the opposite
direction: social media regularly promote mistrust to
such an extent that managers of these platforms have
the increasingly demanding task of removing erroneous
information that perpetuates discord. Facebook and
other social media count users in millions and billions,
which means that more people are publishing more
writing than ever before.

'We are at one of those turning points, for the written
word, that come only rarely in human history,' says
Clayton,

We are witnessing the introduction of new
writing tools and media. It has only happened
twice before, as far as the Roman alphabet is
concerned – once in a process that was several
centuries long, when papyrus scrolls gave way to
vellum books in late antiquity, and again when
Gutenberg invented printing using moveable
type and change swept over Europe in the course
of just one generation, during the late fifteenth
century.

The Spanish writers John of the Cross and Teresa of Avila are the focus of this chapter. They were both writing at a time when the Gutenberg revolution was transforming the way society functioned. As Clayton highlights, there are real parallels between the technological changes of the fifteenth/sixteenth centuries and those of recent decades. These developments changed the 'social technology' of writing by suddenly increasing the availability of texts, via printing in the fifteenth century and via electronic media in the twentieth century. In both these moments of culture shift, readers are challenged by a wave of new writing that poses the question: which writings should we trust? Writing during an era of change touches the reader's original sin of mistrust, either by promoting mistrust or by diminishing it.

Those in authority ask the same question about who to trust, with the added dimension of seeking to control writing they consider harmful. Just as the printed word enabled people to challenge authorities in church and state during the sixteenth century, so social media have empowered people to defy experts and governments in the twenty-first century. The 'social technology' of writing was then as now under strain as people shared contentious insights with an increasingly wide audience. In sixteenth-century Europe, writing about the Reformation led to an increase in mistrust among both those who supported reform and those who opposed it. Yet in the midst of that culture of suspicion, two remarkable writers dared to write about grace in their lives, beyond the limitations of the written language of the day.

ST JOHN OF THE CROSS: *THE SPIRITUAL CANTICLE*

As a 16-year-old studying A-level Spanish, I was given a copy of the poems of St John of the Cross, with parallel translations by Roy Campbell. To my surprise, I could handle the Spanish, especially with help from the translations, whose poetic form mirrored the originals. Here was my very first encounter with the language of grace outside doctrine and liturgy; even my teenage self could tell this was writing of a special kind. At school, I understood the basic language of John's poetry and felt the beauty of his writing, even though I missed many layers of meaning. As part of my university Spanish course, I studied the sixteenth and seventeenth centuries, known as the Golden Age of Spanish literature, and there was John of the Cross again. Here I discovered that John is one of the most admired poets in all Spanish literature, and I began to understand some of the hidden layers in his writing. During my formation as a monk, John was presented to me again, this time as one of the spiritual influences in the refoundation of the English Benedictine Congregation from 1607 onwards after Henry VIII's earlier Dissolution of the Monasteries. As a monk, I discovered that John is a master of the spiritual life. And so it goes on even now: bit by bit I am starting to understand the depths of this extraordinary writer.

Born in 1542 in Old Castille of Catholic parents, he grew up in a simplicity that sometimes slipped into real poverty. From ages 17 to 21 he was a lay student at a school run by the newly formed Jesuit order with a curriculum focused on the humanities, part of the rise of humanism in the Spanish Church at this time. The scholastic approach of previous centuries studied the nature of the divine using philosophical categories and then considered the human. The Renaissance, by contrast, favoured the study of human life as the key to the divine. That is an oversimplification, as both eras sought to harmonize the human and the divine, but it's significant that John of the Cross was a Renaissance man who took seriously the broad study of humanity as a vital part of his understanding of God.

At the age of 20, John entered the Carmelite order of friars and, after a year as a novice, was sent to study philosophy and theology at Salamanca University, one of Europe's leading centres of humanism. There Fray Luis de León taught him how to read the Bible as literature and not simply as a repository of texts to prove Church doctrine. For this unconventional and novel approach, his teacher was denounced to the Inquisition. John's writings are steeped in this same approach to biblical literature; for example, he draws on the *Song of Songs* as the inspiration for one of his greatest poems.

In 1567, John was ordained as a priest and moved to a friary in Medina del Campo, where he met the woman who would transform his life, St Teresa of Avila. A nun of the same Carmelite order as John, Teresa was 27 years older and was embarked on a programme of reforming her order, founding new convents where life was focused on prayer. Within a year John had agreed to initiate the same reform among the friars.

Three events would now shape John's understanding of grace. First, while praying, he had a vison of Christ crucified, and he recorded this vision in a small pen drawing that places the viewer above the cross and slightly to the side. Nobody had ever pictured the crucifixion from such an angle; this is the first indication of the originality of both the life of prayer and the artistic skill of this Renaissance man. Grace manifested in artistry is characteristic of John's writing as well as his drawing. This drawing would become the inspiration for Salvador Dali's 1951 painting *Christ of John of the Cross*, now one of the most popular exhibits in Glasgow's Kelvingrove Gallery.

Alongside this mystical and creative journey, John was actively setting up new, reformed Carmelite communities, which met so much opposition that his superiors imprisoned him in a tiny cell on a penitential diet and had him regularly flogged. This imprisonment was paradoxically another experience of grace; he learned to rely solely on the love of God not passively but by reaching out to seek God in 'an act of pure love'. After eight months he managed to escape, taking with him the third experience of grace, the manuscript of his first poem, *The Spiritual Canticle*. Amid this intense suffering, he began to write poetry; the poem begins by describing a bride in search of her bridegroom:

Esposa:
Adónde te escondiste ...?
Bride:
Where have you hidden
Beloved, and left me moaning?
You fled like the stag

After wounding me:
I went out calling You, and You were gone.

While God is never named in the text, it's clear that
John is drawing on the imagery of the *Song of Songs*:
the Beloved is God and the Bride is the soul. The poem
implies that a brief encounter has left the soul wounded
by divine love yet longing to meet again. Just as a person
can fall in love after a fleeting encounter, so is the soul
in love with God. The soul is now imbued with what
John elsewhere calls 'love's urgent longings'. Yet the
search is at first fruitless: 'and You were gone'.

The 40 stanzas of the *Canticle* describe a conversation
between the Bride and the Groom. As she searches, the
Bride asks the Creatures, 'has He passed by you?' and
they reply:

> Pouring out a thousand graces
> He passed these groves in haste,
> And having looked at them,
> With His image alone
> Clothed them in beauty.

In the final section the Bride says the Bridegroom's beauty
is the place where they will meet and consummate their
love in a consuming but painless fire:

> The breathing of the air,
> The song of the sweet nightingale,
> The grove and its living beauty
> In the serene night,
> With the flame that is consuming and painless.

The final stanza begins, 'No one looked at her,' and there follows a series of mysterious images, whose symbolism John explained years later. The reader is told that Amminadab (a devil) does not appear and the cavalry (the bodily senses) dismount 'at the sight of the waters' (the spiritual goods and delights the soul now knows).

The Carmelite nuns read this poem and asked John to explain it, so he later wrote a lengthy prose commentary in the scholastic style, which he also did for two other poems. Personally, having so enjoyed and been enriched by the poems, I find the prose commentaries harder to enjoy. What John seems to be doing is writing a handbook of mystical experience, using formal, scholastic categories approved by the Church to explain his very human understanding of grace.

As with many great poets, the 'social technology' of John's writing is hard to interpret as he pushes the boundaries of ordinary language. What is distinctive, however, is that his poetry *is* his desire for God, it's not *about* his desire: his poetry is prayer, it's not writing about prayer. In prison, his jailer smuggled in writing materials, and John's writing was a privileged part of the prison experience, indeed the only privileged part. He is writing poetry for himself and for God, nobody else; by contrast, the prose explanations are written for others. Yet if we make the effort to read this writing that takes us to the limits of language, John's poetry passes through the reader 'Pouring out a thousand graces'.

ST JOHN OF THE CROSS: *DARK NIGHT*

John is perhaps best known for his description of the dark night of the soul, a phrase often used today without the speaker knowing its origin or its original meaning. Often it is associated with depression, but what John means is quite different. So let's look at the poem of just 40 short lines that is the origin of the phrase.

> *En una noche oscura ...*
> One dark night,
> Fired with Love's urgent longings,
> – Ah, the sheer grace! –
> I went out unseen,
> My house being now all stilled.

As in the *Canticle*, the soul is searching for the Beloved. The climax is

> Oh, guiding night!
> Oh, night more lovely than the dawn!
> Oh, night that has united
> The Lover with His beloved,
> Transforming the beloved in her Lover.

Clearly, this is a description of ecstasy, not depression. In depression, our faculties grow dark and insensitive, whereas here the faculties are hypersensitive, overwhelmed by a brightness 'more lovely than the dawn'. A parallel is looking directly into the sun: it's so bright that you see nothing. The poet reels back from the brightness and completely reassesses his life; on the first night, his sensual desires are purified, when the inadequacy of worldly pleasure is painfully revealed. The real challenge, however, is the dark night of understanding: the mid-life moment when the poet realizes that his understanding of life is inadequate. In the previous night, he saw through his earthly desires. Now, he sees through his awareness of life itself; he realizes that in fact he knows nothing.

This kind of dark night can be caused by choice (a person gives up everything and goes to serve the destitute), an unavoidable event (a doctor gives a terminal diagnosis) or by natural growth (the diminishments of age lead someone into the depths of the spirit). By whatever means, the dark night is when somebody sees nothing and knows nothing because for the first time the blinding light of the truth about life is seen and understood. The source of this light is not anything that can be described. *Nada,* nothing, is John's favourite, simple word to describe what lies at the peak of the spiritual mountain he sets out to climb. What lies at the summit of true knowledge is nothing like anything else we have ever known. Grace is like nothing we've ever known. No wonder, then, that John's language overflows the banks of the familiar.

This poetry of grace flowed from John's experience of an exceptionally cruel imprisonment. The dark night is dark not because it is about darkness but because we only see the light from a dark place. A parallel is the concept of 'dark sky', the label given to a remote area where there is no light at night so that stars and planets can be seen more clearly. Only from a dark place can the naked eye see the full extent of the Milky Way, the galaxy in which we live. Similarly, the grace in which we live is only fully visible in darkness, the dark night of the soul.

Throughout his life as a friar, John experienced opposition. Even after his death, his supporters had to defend him against misunderstandings and charges of heresy. One defender of John insisted that, if something John wrote appeared not to align with Church doctrine, 'experience conquers doctrine', a bold claim in any era. In 1675, John was beatified by the Pope, eventually canonized and declared a doctor of the Church.

ST TERESA OF AVILA

St Teresa of Avila also featured in my university studies, but in an unexpected part of the syllabus. Her autobiography was part of the linguistics section; we studied it as a key text in the development of written Spanish. *The Life of Mother Teresa of Avila* was among the first texts published in Spain that dealt with serious matters in the day-to-day language of ordinary people; Latin was the language of serious writing, and Spanish was the language of popular stories such as the romances that Teresa tells us she read avidly as a teenager. At the start of the sixteenth century, Latin was for religion, Spanish was for Mills and Boon.

This began to change during Teresa's lifetime. The early sixteenth century saw the publication of some guides to the spiritual life in Spanish, but they used formal Spanish that imitated Latin in order to give them a serious tone. By the middle of the century, however, many of these works in Spanish were banned. The authorities of Church and State were generally nervous about religious texts in Spanish getting into the hands of lay people and hence outside their control; they were especially unsettled by texts dealing with the interior life of the soul. Such writing seemed to challenge the approved, external path of religion, namely, participating in worship, saying traditional prayers and seeking virtue. These external practices could be monitored and controlled, unlike the interior life.

Texts about interior prayer were prime targets in the Spanish Inquisition's campaign to root out three different heresies: Protestantism, Illuminism and Judaism. The ideas of each of these groups were dangerous: Lutheran reformers emphasized the primacy of an individual's faith over the religious works approved by the Church, Illuminists claimed direct inspiration by the Holy Spirit independently of the Church and, following the expulsion of the Jews from Spain in 1492, a cloud hung over the descendants of *conversos,* Jewish families who had converted to Catholicism at that time.

In practice, the Inquisition conflated all three, and Teresa was acutely aware of the danger that the Inquisition would consider her an example of this combination of heresies. Teresa was a reformer, which made her seem Protestant. She had a mystical approach to prayer, which sounded like Illuminism. She was from a Jewish *converso* family. And on top of that she was a woman in a man's world. Her situation was extremely vulnerable to attack by the male hierarchical forces who policed Spain at the time. As one Inquisitor commented on her teaching: she 'passes it off and recommends it as a doctrine revealed by God and inspired by the Holy Spirit; but ... it is a matter contrary to nature for her to have written something taught by an angel, because it exceeds a woman's capacity.'

Teresa published *The Life* in 1565, and the first sentence explains why she was writing:

> Since my confessors commanded me and gave
> me plenty of leeway to write about the favours
> and the kind of prayer the Lord has granted me,
> I wish they would also have allowed me to tell
> very clearly and minutely about my great sins and
> wretched life. This would be a consolation. But
> they didn't want me to.

From the word go, she is downplaying herself. This opening also makes clear that this is not a normal autobiography. It is the story of the Lord's favours to her; it is in some sense a biography of one woman's life of grace. Yet precisely because it is about the graces received, it's very hard to write; the language of grace is not easy to use. 'For a long time, even though God favoured me, I didn't know what words to use to explain His favours: and this was no small trial' (*The Life*, chapter 12). It's also clear that she knew full well the dangers that lurked if she wrote about them in a way that roused the suspicions of the Inquisition. She was clever enough, however, to turn the perceived naivety of her gender to her advantage. Writing about those same favours in the previous chapter, she says: 'As for a poor woman [*mujercita*] like myself, a weak and irresolute creature, it seems right that the Lord should lead me on with favours.' She concludes that learned men don't need such spiritual consolation, and it's annoying that they don't realize this. The learned men didn't spot her use of irony.

Teresa's style of writing about heavenly realities is strikingly down to earth. She wrote, for example, that God can be found among the pots and pans, an image associated with women's domestic work unlikely to cause alarm; yet to find God in daily life is an act of profound interior prayer. This same approach is seen in her description of prayer in *The Life*, where she uses another domestic image, the image of watering a garden. 'We may say that beginners in prayer are those who draw the water up out of the well; which is a great labour.' She works through four images of watering, each stage easier than the last, culminating in the Lord doing all the work by sending rain so that 'the labour is not felt as such, but as bliss.' The final section begins, 'May the Lord teach me words with which to convey some idea of the fourth water.' The grace of prayer takes her to the limits of language, yet once again she plays up her inadequacy.

Teresa writes with a style that could be described as studied confusion, studied because it is a consistent feature of writing by a highly articulate woman, and confusion because that's how she repeatedly describes her own writing. In *The Interior Castle*, when writing about prayer, she exclaims: 'Perhaps everything I say is confused – that's what it feels like, anyway.'

Her self-described confusion is seen, for example, in her use of *pues*, which literally means 'then' but is used in the same way English speakers say 'well' or 'so' to start a sentence. It is uncommon in formal texts, and shows hesitancy while also conveying immediacy. This is how ordinary people speak when they're looking for the right words. Her writing contains the 'um's and 'er's of a conversation.

Confusing too is Teresa's tendency to dash off in a new direction when halfway through explaining something. This can lead to her conflating apparently contradictory ideas or experiences. She was blessed, however, with an editor who understood her writing, the humanist and Bible translator Fray Luis de León, whom we've already met as the teacher of John of the Cross. The Inquisition had imprisoned him for five years as they examined his Spanish translations of the Old Testament for heresy, so he well understood the febrile atmosphere that surrounded Teresa's writings. He commented:

> For even though, in certain passages of what she
> writes, before she completes the sentence that
> she has begun, she contaminates it with other
> sentences and breaks the train of thought, often
> beginning anew with interpolations, nevertheless
> she inserts her digressions so skilfully and
> introduces her fresh thoughts with such grace that
> the defect itself is a source of beauty, like a mole
> on a lovely face.

This did not stop some early copyists and some modern English translators from tidying up her writing to give it a logical sequence that it originally lacked. Such 'corrected' versions fail to convey that the language of grace, like life, has an affective and untidy dimension that refuses to conform to logic. Teresa's prose breaks open language to reshape it so that the words can say new things about the way of grace, a way of writing more usually associated with poetry.

BEING HUMAN, THE WAY TO THE DIVINE

John's poetry and Teresa's prose both flow from the ambiguity and complexity of human nature. Both writers also held firmly to classic Catholic insights about the divine, about the sacraments and about the Church. They saw no contradiction between their humanism and their Catholicism, though they met many Catholics, especially clergy, who contradicted both.

The human path that they trod with such difficulty is the way to God. For them, the meeting place of the human and the divine is a place not only of joy but also of suffering. Teresa wrote of the 'pain of love', and describes this in *The Life* most memorably in an experience of prayer known as the Ecstasy of St Teresa.

It seemed to me this angel plunged the dart
several times into my heart and that it reached
deep within me ... The pain was so great that it
made me moan, and the sweetness this greatest
pain caused me was so superabundant that there
is no desire capable of taking it away ... the loving
exchange that takes place between the soul and

God is so sweet that I beg Him in His goodness
to give a taste of this love to anyone who thinks I
am lying. (*The Life*, chapter 29)

I have still not quite recovered from the experience when
I was aged 19 of entering the chapel of Teresa's convent
in Avila and seeing this description carved in stone; my
studies hadn't got as far as this text, and I was reading it for
the first time. I was travelling round Spain with a friend
who didn't speak Spanish, so I gave him a spontaneous
translation, at the end of which I was speechless, and he
simply said: 'I wonder what Freud would make of that?'
That's the point: it is clearly erotic and clearly spiritual.
Unlike John, whose prose explains the imagery of the
Lover and the Beloved in more analytic terms, Teresa
never wrote a scholastic explanation of these experiences.
Her words simply sit there, a challenge to the language
that would contain grace in categories and rituals.

The writing of John and Teresa is original artistry;
that's to say, in terms of the history of written Spanish,
they broke barriers and generated new forms of writing
that are still admired for their creativity by believers and
non-believers alike. Through their writing they reveal
grace to their readers as something active in their own
lives.

There are parallels with those who 'write' icons, this
being the term used for the act of creating an icon in
the Orthodox tradition of the Eastern Church. Icon
writers are governed by clear guidelines, and guidance
makes their work a spiritual activity. A medieval text
called *The Rules for the Icon Painter* begins

1 Before starting work, make the sign of the
   Cross, pray in silence and pardon your
   enemies.
2 Work with care on every detail of your icon
   as if you were working in front of the Lord
   himself.

These are not so much craft rules as instructions about
how to pray when at work on the icon culminating in:

9. Never forget the joy of spreading icons in the
world.

That same attitude imbues the poetry of John and the
prose of Teresa. They don't tell us about grace. Like icon
writers, they show us grace. Such writing is a reminder
that Christian living isn't an ideology – that's to say, it
isn't a system that people can adopt to save themselves
and the world. Their writing takes readers by the hand
and describes what it's like to plunge into the depths of
being human, confident that in God's own time and
not before, the divine will be revealed there. John of
the Cross's *The Spiritual Canticle* and *The Life of Mother
Teresa of Avila* are not written as systems to follow; they
are the creative outpouring of souls who broke open
ordinary language in order to express their own intense
spiritual experiences, transforming it into the language
of grace.

Bookshops today are full of systems that promote
well-being, and there is much good in them. But just as
the language of grace can be distorted by shoving it into

prescribed categories, so it can be distorted by equating it with the language of well-being. The tendency to equate spirituality with healthy living obscures the reality of grace as divine gift.

At the start of this chapter, I explained why this is a critical moment in the history of writing: the challenge is to encourage fresh creative artists to write the language of grace for this era of culture shift. The Christian grime artist Stormzy is a rock star who clearly knows the language of contemporary culture and its many formats. At the same time, he has a lot to say about grace, as seen in the lyrics of 'Blinded by Your Grace, Pts 1 and 2'. His personal life is not that of a member of a religious order, and he has admitted some of his past actions were wrong. Yet on the Glastonbury Festival Main Stage in 2019, broadcast live by the BBC, he sang about grace in his own life and touched millions of people. His lyrics have the logic-defying, broken quality of the Spanish mystics, and his writing communicates the same sense of the immediacy of grace, drawing on his own experiences of brokenness and redemption. He uses an image that mirrors that found in John's *Dark Night*, namely, the writer's inability to see because he's blinded by grace. There are many reasons why Stormzy is not a modern John of the Cross, not least because his theology appears to come from an Evangelical rather than a Catholic foundation. Nevertheless, the parallels are striking: a widely acclaimed artistry with words used to describe the effects of God's grace in his own life, in ways that disturb both the secular and the religious consensus about the way religion should be treated: the liberal consensus that religion has no place on a public stage and the religious conventions that religion has certain official channels that don't look like Stormzy.

'WE DO NOT WRITE TO BE UNDERSTOOD; WE WRITE TO UNDERSTAND' (C. DAY LEWIS)

John of the Cross began to write poetry in prison as part of his prayer. A similar impulse lies behind the writing of the psalms: the *Book of Psalms* in the Hebrew Bible is a collection of writings that are the heartfelt outpourings of Jewish people from past centuries that echo in the hearts of many people today, Jews and gentiles, believers and non-believers. It may seem that people write down prayers so that God can understand how a person is feeling and what they need. Yet to put it that way already shows how this can't really be the reason; the God of Abraham is all-knowing, so already knows all about us and our needs. The point of writing down prayers is not to help God understand us, but to help the writer move closer to God.

The saint of the English Reformation, Thomas More, wrote the following prayer:

> Give to us, O God, a heart transformed by grace and a life inspired by humility. Grant us fullness of faith, firmness of hope and fervency of love. Let our one desire be conformity to your perfect will: through Christ our Lord. Amen.

This prayer helps the one praying it to focus on the essentials: the desire to be transformed by grace and live humbly, and the need to seek faith, hope and love, qualified by the lovely trio of fullness, firmness and fervour, culminating in a version of 'Thy will be done.' As More wrote, it was God's Spirit that was praying in him; the writer was concentrating on that presence and describing how he experienced that prayer of the Holy Spirit in him, namely as 'a heart transformed by grace'. As St Paul says, 'The Spirit helps us in our weakness; for we do not know how to pray as we ought, but that very Spirit intercedes with sighs too deep for words.'

St Teresa used to shake the hourglass to make her half hour of prayer go more quickly. The greatest challenge in a time of prayer is to stay focused on the Spirit's deep sighs. A written prayer is an attempt to turn the divine sighs beyond words into a human form that helps both the writer and those who pray it to stay focused. The grace of prayer is a circular flow that begins with God's Spirit, not us, and well-composed words can help us stay with the flow. If God is all-knowing, then God has already factored that prayer into the divine response, which is why it's important for a person to say the words.

Not many of us are as gifted at writing as Teresa or John, Thomas More or the psalmist, or Stormzy. Yet we too can really benefit from writing. For example, I have on occasion kept a journal for several months to help me make an important decision. By making myself write a discernment journal over a certain period, I focus on what's involved. So too with writing a prayer. If I want to pray for somebody or some intention, the act of writing it down helps me to understand just what it is I'm praying for.

Writing is, then, a source of grace that helps people to understand themselves, their neighbours and God, which is why the written language of grace matters. If somebody writes with grace on social media, they're building trust between users. If a person writes a prayer for their personal use, they're focusing their trust in God. If a refugee writes a cry of despair then others may respond. The possibilities are endless. Such writing shows our interdependence and builds trust, the language of grace that overcomes the original sin of mistrust.

WRITING EXERCISES

Write your own journal of grace. This could be noticing each day where you experienced trust from others and gave it to others. Or maybe something 'came to you in a flash' – notice when you're blinded by grace.

Write your own psalm. Address God directly and lovingly. Then write down your joys and hopes, your griefs and anxieties. Conclude by thanking God.

On the BBC Music YouTube channel search for Stormzy at Glastonbury 2019 singing 'Blinded by Your Grace, Pt 2'. How do you respond to his words and his performance? The lyrics in written form are easily accessible by searching online. Perhaps write your own response imitating his style.

5

Reading

Blessed is anyone who reads the words of this prophecy.

Rev. *1.3*

WAYS OF READING

Visiting Jerusalem some years ago, I went to the Church of the Holy Sepulchre, the location of Christ's tomb. This site is both sacred and a source of conflict, as different Christian denominations dispute their respective rights of access to different parts of a complex set of buildings. Every inch of the building is argued over. Ethiopian Coptic monks have an ancient foothold on the roof of the Church so, leaving behind the general tourist noise in the church itself, I was pleased to find serenity on the roof. Sitting there in the shade, an Ethiopian monk was holding a large, old book in both hands; he was reading it out loud – to himself. I was mesmerized by his reading, because this was the nearest I'd ever come to hearing – yes, hearing – the way that was for centuries the normal way of reading.

In his *Confessions,* St Augustine describes his first meeting with the Bishop of Milan, St Ambrose around AD 385. As he entered the room, Augustine found the bishop reading. 'When he read, his eyes scanned the page and his heart sought out the meaning, but his voice was silent and his tongue was still.' That's a good description of how a book will usually be read nowadays. Augustine goes on to say that whenever he visited Ambrose 'we found him reading like this in silence, for he never read aloud.' Silent reading was so unusual in the fourth century that it was noteworthy.

For Augustine and his classical predecessors, letters were what he called 'signs of sounds', and those sounds were 'signs of things we think'. The process of reading went from written word to sound to thought, whereas most people today go from writing to thought without sounding out the words in between. The greatest authors, however, have never forgotten the importance of the sound of words that will be read. The French nineteenth-century novelist Gustave Flaubert is famous for the skill with which his sentences are constructed. At the end of each day's writing, he would take his manuscript and read it out loud to his maid. He needed to hear what he'd written as a way of checking its quality and to ensure its clarity. 'Prose, like verse', he said 'must be written so that it can be read out loud. Poorly written sentences never pass the test: they tighten the chest and impede the beating of the heart.'

Schools also know this. The youngest children are taught to read by reading out loud; for older students, reading a text out loud in class is a standard way of learning its meaning. Or take the instinctive way people read out loud in private a text that is not immediately understood, such as a complex contract, or which they need to follow very carefully, such as a new recipe. The sight of somebody in their kitchen reading out loud the cooking instructions from a packet passes unnoticed, while a commuter on a train reading the newspaper out loud would cause as much astonishment today as Ambrose's silent reading did in the fourth century.

Beyond educational settings, reading out loud to oneself continues to be appreciated, but only in limited circumstances: reading poetry out loud for the private pleasure of the sounds or reading out a passage to assess its quality. Sadly, the skill of public reading is not so highly valued, and is generally at a low level of competence these days. That last comment is based on my own experience of presiding at weddings and funerals, where well-intentioned but nervous friends and relatives ruin the reading of a sacred text. Occasionally at one of these services, however, I am taken by surprise, and listen with delight to somebody reading from the Bible in a way that lifts the heart and mind of the hearer, a true moment of grace.

REASONS FOR READING

All three kinds of reading discussed so far can be moments of grace: silent reading, reading out loud on one's own and public reading. Each in their different way has the potential to be a peak experience of the language of grace. For example, the Catholic Church teaches that 'He [Christ] is present in His word, since it is He Himself who speaks when the holy scriptures are read in the Church.' To hear a public reading of the Bible during a service is, Catholics believe, a privileged moment of encounter with the language of grace. As we will see, something of this can also be found in the private reading of scripture approached in a particular way. Similarly, for some people reading a poem to themselves can be a moment of consolation in grief or an expression of joy in spring.

While many people would notice poor reading in public by another person, they might not have a similar critical awareness of their own private reading. For private reading to be a moment of grace requires an approach that is out of kilter with some contemporary ideas about what constitutes good reading.

For example, speed reading is seen as a positive skill that can be learnt by joining a course, usually at a price. This assumes good reading is measured 'by the yard', so to speak; the quicker you read, the more text you can consume, and the more you will learn. People who have studied at college or university will have found themselves 'skim' reading to meet deadlines. That is a kind of speed reading learnt through necessity.

Another activity that isn't always conducive to gracious reading is textual analysis, where every word and phrase is examined to consider its meaning. This approach can provide new insights and helpful background to a text, but it can also kill a text stone dead. The reading of a Shakespeare play can, for example, be a wonderfully inspiring part of secondary education, but over-analysis of the text can have a deadening effect. This approach has been compared to killing a beautiful butterfly in order to study it. The same problem arises in biblical studies. In both cases, the desire to achieve detailed textual understanding can become an obstacle to aesthetic and spiritual appreciation. To be clear, the Shakespearian aesthetic and biblical spirituality are quite distinct, but the personal appreciation of both can be hindered by excessive analysis. Equally, the enjoyment of both can be heightened by approaching them as channels of grace.

The effect a book has on a reader is largely determined by whether the text meets the expectations of the reader. For example, if someone reads a travel guide for information about a town, they will be pleased to find accurate information. If the same person is on holiday and reads a novel based in the same town, they will enjoy its local references even if some of the town details are inaccurate. A travel guide with too many stories and a novel full of travel facts will both defy expectations and leave the reader feeling disappointed.

The different kinds of reading noted so far are generally determined by the different reasons someone has for reading. Nowadays the most widespread incentives for reading are probably reading for information and reading for recreation. These two incentives can be combined with two techniques: speed and analysis. So people will tend to speed-read the front page of a newspaper but may then read a feature article more carefully; the reader combines speed and analysis to obtain information.

Similarly, somebody reading a thriller may read the set-up of the plot carefully but then find themselves turning the pages quickly to get to the thrilling climax. Both analysis and speed can be used to enhance the pleasing recreation people find in thrillers.

Grace as a motive for reading is something most people cannot easily understand, yet it used to be the primary motivation of all serious reading. One of the last great exponents of this way of reading was Hugh of St Victor, a teacher in twelfth-century Paris. For him, the motive for reading was neither information nor recreation but to help the reader in their search for wisdom. In the *Didascalicon*, he outlined what we would call a curriculum for his students; its opening words are: 'Of all things to be sought, the first is wisdom.' As a Christian, Hugh believed that the source of all wisdom is the Word of God made visible in Christ. He offered his students Christ as 'the Form, the Medicine, the Example, He is your remedy.' Just as a doctor prescribes a medicine from the pharmacopeia at his disposal, so a wise guide prescribes a verse from scripture as a remedy for the ills of the soul.

The healing power of such reading was part of medieval life. The learned and literate master of arts could pass on his wisdom to others – sometimes just one or two verses of scripture to meet the person's particular situation at the time. This was 'a word to live by', so that even somebody who was illiterate could memorize and 'read' these words. This echoed the world's oldest known library motto dating from the second millennium BC; an ancient Greek history tells us that over the door of the library of Rameses the Great in Egypt was inscribed: 'The house of healing for the soul'.

In Hugh's view of reading, there are only two 'books' worth reading: the book of salvation, the Bible, and the book of nature, the arts and sciences. Until the twelfth century, Christian Europe saw all reading as the learning of wisdom, whether the text was sacred or secular. Arts and sciences were to be learnt precisely because they were seen as describing God's creation and hence, like scripture, they can be a remedy for our souls. There is no separation of sacred learning and secular learning; there is only learning for wisdom. Reading is a holistic activity where sacred and secular are one. To read a text of arts or sciences is to be primarily engaged in the work of your salvation and only secondarily, if at all, in the acquiring of information.

Those who founded the universities in the thirteenth century began a process which led to a different aim: they began to seek information about the world for its own sake, and then started to analyse it. This analytic approach dissected the world and reading followed suit; reading was for understanding and controlling life, not for receiving wisdom. Sacred and secular separated, and only religious reading was considered sacred. So reading became primarily the very functional activity that it is today: reading for information and control, with reading for recreation a close second.

Yet during the twentieth century a version of the medieval tradition of reading as remedy began to emerge. It started as a library service for soldiers hospitalized during the First World War, whose well-being was improved by reading books. After the war, this developed into choosing books that suited somebody's health condition, and became known as bibliotherapy, or more colloquially reading for health. There are today reading for health groups in major hospitals around the world. In one British hospital the leader of the programme favours reading out loud in a group as having benefits beyond those of belonging to an ordinary social group. In America in 1980, the National Association for Poetry Therapy brought together many practitioners and began publishing the *Journal for Poetry Therapy*. The mental and physical health benefits of reading are now well established – not just any reading, however, but the kind of reading that fosters health, hence the development of bibliotherapy as a skill.

A BBC Radio 5 Live initiative in 2021 invited listeners to send in recordings of themselves reading aloud a text that was special to them. The reasons stated on their website for this project are striking. 'We'll be exploring the potential benefits of reading aloud, such as improving memory, bringing communities together and helping people with low literacy gain confidence.' Memory skills, community building, confidence raising; the language of grace indeed.

READING FOR GRACE

My life is shaped by the Rule of St Benedict, the sixth-century guide for monks and the foundation of life in all Benedictine and Cistercian monasteries to this day.

One aspect of the Rule that surprises modern readers is that when Benedict uses the word 'meditate' he is referring to a way of reading, not a technique for stilling the mind. Techniques to achieve mindfulness are very popular today; such techniques can be very beneficial, but Benedict offers no such techniques. This is partly because Benedict assumes three traditions of meditation that were already established parts of monastic life by his time; they were in some sense a contemporary version of mindfulness. As will be seen, however, these add up to a way of life rather than a technique.

The first is the tradition of the hours or offices when monks gather in church six or seven times a day to recite psalms, to listen to readings and to pray for God's help. The psalms are usually chanted, a form of communal reading out loud set to simple music that is both worship and communal meditation. Benedict calls this the *opus dei*, the work of God, as he sees it as the strongest way of prayer.

The second monastic tradition Benedict assumes is that of the repeated phrase as a basic way of praying: the monk takes a line from the psalms such as 'Be still and know that I am God' or 'Lord Jesus, have mercy on me, a sinner.' The monk repeats this phrase constantly in his mind or out loud to help him stay focused on God. The long-term goal of the monastic life is to 'see God' based on the saying of Jesus: 'Blessed are the pure in heart for they shall see God.' This purity of heart is achieved by constant prayer, and hence the repeated phrase. This approach to meditation has been described as heartfulness rather than mindfulness; the mind is emptied of mundane concerns, as in mindfulness, but this is pursued not for its own sake but as the gateway to a pure heart and heartfelt love.

Alongside public prayer and interior prayer is the final tradition that Benedict inherited known as *lectio divina*. Literally translated this means 'divine reading', but a better translation is 'meditative reading'. This way of reading is what Benedict means when he uses the word 'meditation'. Meditative reading is at the heart of Christian monasticism. As already mentioned, books were rare events until the invention of printing, but monasteries had to have texts available for monks to engage in meditative reading. In some poor monasteries, the library was what we would now consider a large cupboard where the sacred texts were stored and often carefully handed out to monks by the abbot. In richer monasteries, there might be larger libraries, but the aim of such collections was always the study of holy wisdom in scripture and in nature.

This approach contrasts starkly with today's norm of fast, analytic reading for information or distraction. 'Meditative reading' always involves a sacred text, but it is not only the contents but also the way of reading that is distinctive. The text is read slowly, an approach that is difficult for modern readers and needs to be consciously acquired by novices entering monastic life.

This approach has been compared to the four stages of eating food. First, the text is bitten off by reading it once. Then it is chewed over through repetition. After that, the words are swallowed a piece at a time as the significance of a word or phrase is savoured. Finally, the whole text sits in the stomach as the eater/reader silently enjoys the satisfaction of a good feed/a good read and contemplates the goodness of God. Typically, this approach takes 20 to 30 minutes to read a sacred text of between 150 and 200 words, which would take about two minutes to read at a normal modern speed.

The aim of this book, however, is not to dwell on the language of grace as used in an explicitly religious context such as *lectio divina*. The purpose of describing that approach is as a contrast, to highlight how contemporary approaches to reading are a choice. People today choose to read for information and for distraction; sometimes they speed-read and sometimes they read carefully. In general, they have learnt these ways of reading at a young age so that the way they read is instinctive. They are not aware that they are making unconscious choices about how they read.

The lifelong unlearning described in the first chapter applies here as well. Just as everybody has the challenge of unlearning mistrust to overcome what Christians call original sin, so too readers today can unlearn their compulsion to read quickly for information or distraction. These two unlearnings, of fast reading and of mistrust, can be united. A reader can choose to read a text as if it were medicine or a remedy to cure the ills of the soul.

Certain forms demand careful reading. Poetry insists on being read slowly for at least two reasons: first, the sense of a poem is often not obvious, and secondly, the beauty of the phrasing invites the reader to savour the words. William Blake's 'The Tyger' is a good example.

Tyger, tyger burning bright,
In the forests of the night,
What immortal hand or eye,
Could frame thy fearful symmetry?

The first two lines almost demand to be savoured and read aloud simply because they sound so good. Their rhythm and rhyme are perfect. And the whole stanza invites the reader to pause and imagine a tiger. The four subsequent stanzas develop the portrait of this magnificent wild beast. The final stanza is the same as the first, with one word changed, the final two lines of the poem read:

What immortal hand or eye,
Dare frame thy fearful symmetry?

Is the one who dares the figure seen in Blake's coloured etching *The Ancient of Days*, the primeval figure bending over the void with a pair of compasses? The critic Tom Paulin has noted that, when Blake wrote this poem, 'the tiger was frequently used as an emblem of the revolutionary Paris mob.' So there may be a political undertone asking who dared to unleash this beast of revolution. Even without these wider insights, the poem is a delight to read out loud and ponder. Blake was a nonconformist in every sense, so he, like the Spanish mystics, was pushing language to its limits to convey his understanding of grace within his very distinctive, Deist cosmology. His paintings and his poetry demand a meditative approach if they are to be appreciated.

READING *GILEAD*

The same is true of some prose writing, especially some novels. So in this section I want to look at the works of Marilynne Robinson, whose Gilead series of novels are outstanding examples of secular writing that radiates grace. Writing in *The New Yorker*, the unbelieving Mark O'Connell commented, 'I have read and loved a lot of literature about religion and religious experience –Tolstoy, Dostoevsky, Flannery O'Connor, the Bible – but it's only with Robinson that I have actually felt what it must be like to live with a sense of the divine.' In an era when much of Western culture sees religion as dangerous or at best irrelevant, Robinson has a rare capacity to connect with the heart of the literary establishment, winning the Pulitzer Prize for Fiction in 2005 for *Gilead* and the Orange Prize for Fiction in 2009 for *Home*.

My encounter with her work began by reading her second novel, *Gilead,* the first of the series of the same name. While reading the first 40 pages or so, it dawned on me that I was reading with the same sense of grace as I had known when reading *The Diary of a Country Priest,* a French Catholic novel by Georges Bernanos. To my astonishment, just as this thought came to me, the text mentioned that very book. Both works contain a highly personal account of the life of a pastor, one Catholic, the other Protestant. John Ames, pastor of the fictitious town of Gilead, expresses admiration for the story of the French priest. *The Diary* tells the story of the Curé of Ambricourt (we never learn his name), despised by both rich and poor parishioners; he dies of consumption in the arms of a disgraced confrère who has fathered a child out of wedlock. The book concludes with the sentence: '*Tout est grâce,*' 'All is grace,' the catch phrase of St Thérèse of Lisieux. The story of a priest dying in the midst of a family comprising a defrocked priest, an unmarried mother and an illegitimate child shocked Catholic sensibility when the book was published in 1936. To conclude by affirming that here too grace is present added to that shock, especially using a phrase associated with the popular piety of the saint known as the Little Flower. Again and again, the most creative Christian authors describe grace turning up in the wrong place.

When Marilynne Robinson was asked if she was consciously influenced by the Catholic novel tradition, she gently batted the question away by saying that she read widely and that all novels with a religious theme interested her. While she doesn't accept any explicit influence from the Catholic novel tradition, her writing does have a similar feel, which is surprising given that she explicitly describes herself as an admirer of John Calvin, the great Protestant reformer. Her characters sometimes refer to Calvinism, but more importantly they show us Calvin's understanding of grace in action. Contrary to the popular notion of Calvinism as puritanical and exclusive, Robinson's novels are underpinned by a Calvinism that offers a generous and inclusive grace.

To illustrate Robinson's Calvinist humanism, I will look at just one of the Gilead novels, the fourth and most recent, *Jack*. This is the story of the eponymous Jack's simultaneous disgrace and redemption. The four novels each stand on their own, but the central characters remain the same as one or other takes turns to be centre stage in each book. From the earlier novels, the reader learns that Jack is the black sheep of the family of Pastor Boughton, a colleague of Pastor Ames. Jack left Gilead in disgrace having fathered an illegitimate child whose mother died. This novel finds him in 1950s St Louis, unemployed and almost unemployable, surviving on his wits, which are extensive and ingenious. *Jack* opens with some short sections that introduce the reader to the fraught relationship between Jack and Della, a schoolteacher, whom we soon realize is a woman of colour. The next 70 pages describe a chance encounter between the two in a cemetery where Jack was hoping to spend the night and where Della became stranded, having miscalculated the closing time. The sharp, witty and sad dialogue between them leaves the reader struggling to grasp what's going on, but with a deep sense that underneath this bizarre conversation something significant is growing between them. The rest of the book unfolds that something into a moving story of forbidden love across a racial divide.

The anti-hero Jack is the high point of grace in the Gilead series just as much as he is the low point of unacceptable behaviour; he is the great sinner completely saved by grace. The way the author leads us though this paradox is pure delight because there is joy throughout, even as everything goes wrong. In one of the earlier Gilead novels, *Lila,* Pastor Ames says, 'Grace has a grand laughter about it.' Laughter and delight are serious dimensions of Robinson's novels, and never more so than in *Jack.*

One of Jack's recurring aspirations is to be harmless, yet he finds that harming others follows relentlessly in his wake no matter how hard he tries. As he says of himself: 'I'm a bum, without aspirations or illusions.' Jack's bottom line is that he can't help himself. And that is why his life is such an eloquent expression of grace. Crucially, he isn't an addict or a criminal, so this is not a gangs-to-gospel story as found in some evangelical preaching and writing. The famous evangelical hymn begins by affirming 'Amazing Grace!/ How sweet the sound/ That saved a wretch like me.' Jack is such a wretch not because he is up to no good, but just by virtue of who is. He is the human condition writ large: individual people cannot save themselves from making mistakes. This is often characterized in Calvinist theology as the total depravity of all human beings. Jack's character says the same thing in less austere terms.

Jack's profound self-knowledge means he can name his failings, recognize his inability to change them and embrace even the smallest sign of grace. Self-knowledge is an important part of the language of grace, because if a person cannot recognize their own failings or depravity there is no room for grace. In the popular imagination, this sense of failure leads to Catholic guilt about specific actions. In the world of Gilead, however, there is a lightness of touch about accepting that to be human is to be corrupt. Jack knows he has done terrible things (the memory of abandoning the woman who bore their illegitimate child is a recurring source of shame), yet they do not crush him. He never stops trying to be harmless, but he is not surprised when he fails; this is not a licence to sin but rather the basis of his welcoming the grace that keeps saving him.

This grace comes especially from Della's love for him. Their relationship is not only forbidden by the racist laws of the time, but it also crosses class lines; she is a high school teacher and the daughter of a bishop, he an unemployed bum and the disgraced son of a pastor. Jack's continuous facility for causing harm is met by Della's endless capacity to love. Her love is all the more gracious for being so unexpected and so undeserved. The mystery of her love illustrates the mystery of what Calvinists call irresistible grace: Della's love cannot be refused because it simply overwhelms Jack.

Their relationship also exemplifies the Calvinist idea of unconditional election. Grace is not distributed by God on the basis of merit; it is not a reward for the righteous but a gift to a self-proclaimed 'ne'er-do-well' like Jack. He is one of those predestined (another favourite Calvinist idea) to be saved no matter how undeserving.

Where Robinson parts company with a strict version of Calvinism is in her belief that, as she has said at interview, 'if you see the grace of God as fully sufficient there is no exclusion left in the Resurrection.' She went on to say: 'Most formulae of salvation don't include the mass of humanity.' The notion that the gift of grace is limited to certain people is one interpretation of Calvin, but this is not something she appears to accept. She implies that everybody is predestined to receive the grace of salvation, but doesn't feel the need to work through some of the complex arguments about free will and predestination that have surrounded this topic for centuries. Occasionally predestination is mentioned and is the subject of a sustained discussion in *Gilead*. When it is first mentioned Pastor Ames comments, 'That is probably my least favourite topic of conversation in the entire world,' a sentiment I suspect that is Robinson's own. Jack is part of that conversation in this earlier book, and he presses those present to explain whether people can change if they are predestined to damnation or salvation. 'I'm not going to force some theory on a mystery and make foolishness of it,' insists Ames, 'just because that is what people who talk about it normally do.' Towards the end of the discussion Jack's father, Pastor Boughton, says, 'To conclude is not in the nature of the enterprise.' Robinson leaves the topic there, with no conclusion. Yet she can't quite leave it alone, and it emerges again in passing during a conversation in *Jack*.

The insight that predestination brings to the character of Jack is that he just is the way that he is, with good points and bad points; he can't judge whether the good or the bad is dominant, which gives him an engaging lightness of spirit and detachment from worldly ambition. As Robinson has commented, Jack can't live within social structures; he is not defiant, just untouched by convention, and in that sense pure. This Calvinist humanism insists that a person's nature is given, not made, and that, by virtue of its being given, it is a gift, specifically a gift of grace. This is the Protestant challenge that *Jack* presents not only to Catholic 'works' (a term full of Reformation controversy) that make someone holy, but also to the modern belief that 'man makes himself.'

Marilynne Robinson does not so much write about these matters as weave them into the text. As we read, we are not simply engaging with ideas but above all feeling the force of them in the act of reading. This is not *lectio divina* where the reading is purposely repetitive to savour a sacred text. But it is spiritual reading, because a Robinson novel forces a slow reading pace; the text demands close attention if it is to be grasped and allowed to touch the reader's life. This can be compared with looking at a great painting; it can be glanced at just as *Jack* can be subjected to speed reading, but glancing and speed reading would both miss the whole experience of a great work of art: to enjoy the details and the depth of what is shown, leading the viewer/reader to an insight and an experience that they had not known before.

In *Jack*, this is illustrated most clearly in the book's final paragraph. By this stage, Jack and Della have found a way to live together despite the law and Jack is being transformed by Della's unconditional love. This paragraph, and indeed the last word, sum up not only the theme of the novel itself but also the theme of this book. Above all, the style forced me to read this paragraph more than once and out loud to myself in order to fully grasp what was being said, because at first I didn't spot the reference to Genesis. Is it a spoiler to show you the whole of this joyful concluding section? Not really, because the pleasure of this book is not in coming to the end of a story but in the reading and the re-reading of grace at work throughout the story. Here it is:

The knowledge of the good. That half of the primal
catastrophe received too little attention. Guilt and
grace met together in that phrase despite all that.
He could think of himself as a thief sneaking off
with an inestimable wealth of meaning and trust,
all of it offended and damaged beyond use, except
to remind him of the nature of the crime. Or he
could consider the sweet marriage that made her a
conspirator with him in it, the loyalty that always
restored them both, just like grace.

READING EXERCISES

Try any or all of the following and notice how you react
to them.

Lectio Divina: Using the description of *Lectio*
compared to eating on p. 105, try reading in this way
using a text from the Bible or another source that is
sacred to you.

Reading out loud: Choose a poem or piece of prose
that you like and read it out loud in private.

Notice and extend your reading activity: As your day
unfolds, notice the different kinds of reading you use. If
it helps, keep a journal of how many different approaches
to reading you use over a week. Then consider being more
intentional in the following week and include new kinds
of reading; you may not usually do these, so consider
including them: slow reading of poetry, spiritual reading
of a great work of literature; joining a reading group.

6

Reading the Situation

*You know how to read the face of the sky, can
you not read the signs of the times?*

Mt. 16.3

LANGUAGE BEYOND WORDS

'Are there languages to think in other than the ones
in which we talk?' asks Robert Bringhurst in *The Tree
of Meaning*. 'And the answer is. Of course! There are
the languages of mathematics, the languages of music,
languages of colour, shape and gesture. Language is
what something becomes when you think in it.'

In this final chapter, I'll be looking at how we
communicate with more than words, starting with how
people can read the language of situations and see there
grace or its absence. For example, 'What's your reading
of the situation?' is a perfectly normal question to ask
somebody, but what is a person doing when they read
a situation?

Reading the situation is exactly what Jesus was doing when he asked his contemporaries, 'Can't you read the signs of the times?' The Jewish religious leaders were testing Jesus; they wanted him to show them a sign from heaven to prove his credentials as a prophet. His reply implies that they were wasting their time with trick questions about signs from heaven when the signs all around them showed that their situation as leaders in Israel was under threat. 'Don't ask me to give you a new sign to show you I'm a prophet,' he seemed to say. 'My prophesy is to point out what's already going on around you.' He pointed out that everybody knows how to read the weather: red sky in the evening, good weather; red sky in the morning, bad weather. If you can read the signs in the sky, why can't you read the signs of the times that are under your nose?

Jesus may have been referring to the political situation of the time and the imminent fate of those same Jewish leaders who were quizzing him. The Romans were growing weary of Jewish rebellions, and irritated by Jewish religious disputes that disturbed the *pax romana*. In AD 44, Jewish rule in Israel came to an end as Rome took back control from the dynasty of the Herods. Following a Jewish revolt against Roman rule in AD 66, the Romans responded with fierce repression and the destruction of the Jerusalem temple in AD 70. Jesus had read the situation correctly. His questioners should watch out for the signs around them, and not ask for new ones; looking at the Temple he had said: 'All these things you see – the time will come when not a single stone will be left on another which will not be pulled down'. (Lk. 21.6)

These reading skills of Jesus are significant ways of reading languages other than those that are found in texts. The signs of the times can be read, and there grace can be found.

In the Hebrew tradition, prophets are people who see into the future not by magic but by their ability to read the signs of the times in the present. The typical shape of such prophesy went something like this: if people go on acting as they are then there will be a disaster in the future. If you rob the poor and short-change your customers, for example, then you will lose God's favour and be punished. Or, if you make an alliance against an enemy with one of Israel's pagan neighbours, don't be surprised if the alliance turns sour so that you are betrayed by your neighbour and defeated by your enemy. In the area of political alliances, the prophet and the king are usually at odds: the ruler is concerned about the immediate security of the kingdom through short-term alliances, but the prophet looks to the future, saying this will turn out badly in the long run. There are echoes of this ancient clash in the current quarrels between politicians and environmental activists: governments must secure the immediate energy needs of their people, but environmentalists warn that this is unsustainable without a major change in the way the energy is produced. The kings and the prophets are at loggerheads today as in the past. The books of the prophets insist a prophet must be heeded, but those same books also describe false prophets. The challenge is to discern the true from the false prophet.

It's tempting to listen to the prophets who speak words of consolation and to ignore those who deliver jeremiads, a word derived from the name Jeremiah, the gloomiest of the Hebrew prophets. Some army officers put Jeremiah down a well to keep him quiet. The harder truth is that prophesy is often the bringer of grace when it tells truths that people don't want to hear. There is, however, another way into prophesy that bypasses the choice between a prophesy being either good news or bad news. The language of a prophet can be so original and creative that it reveals a new sphere of life where the good/bad split is overwhelmed by a new way of being, a way where death and resurrection are two sides of one coin. The connection between death and resurrection is a pattern embedded in life and in the Easter mystery. To uncover this feature of life requires a prophetic language that reveals hidden dimensions of grace. So I turn now to a poet who did this with astonishing and courageous originality.

GLORIOUS LANGUAGE

Gerard Manley Hopkins (1844–89) was a poet and Jesuit priest whose genius was only recognized posthumously. He is one of the founders of modern poetry, as he set aside the conventions of Victorian poetic language to create a new way of writing. He was educated within those conventions, and studied the great romantic poets, especially Keats, but he was critical of them, and of Keats in particular, saying of him: 'His contemporaries ... still concerned themselves with great causes [such] as liberty and religion, but he lived in mythology and fairyland, the life of a dreamer.' Hopkins learned from the Romantics how to describe nature, but he wanted to write poetry of a different kind. This break with tradition was his clear intention, as is seen in correspondence with his friend, the poet Robert Bridges. 'The effect of studying masterpieces is to make me admire,' he wrote, 'and do otherwise.'

How his new way of writing came about is best told in his own words:

> What I had written I burned before I became
> a Jesuit and resolved to write no more, as not
> belonging to my profession, unless it were by the
> wish of my superiors; so for seven years I wrote
> nothing but two or three little presentation pieces
> which occasion called for. But when in the winter
> of '75 the *Deutschland* was wrecked in the mouth
> of the Thames and five Franciscan nuns, exiles
> from Germany by the Falck Laws, aboard of her
> were drowned, I was affected by the account and
> happening to say so to my rector he said that
> he wished someone would write a poem on the
> subject. On this hint I set to work and, though
> my hand was out at first, produced one. I had
> long had haunting my ear the echo of a new
> rhythm which now I realized on paper.

In 'The Wreck of the *Deutschland*' Hopkins writes not only with what he called *sprung rhythm*, but also in a new style that abandoned normal sentence structure. That left some of his contemporaries bemused. Hopkins realized that this new way of writing was not going to be popular. In another letter to Bridges he commented: 'If you do not like it [my music] it is because there is something you have not seen and I see.' What is striking is his emphasis on what he sees; the first step in his poetry is that he reads the world differently to other people. To describe what he sees requires him to disrupt ordinary language, reshaping its rhythm and structure to describe the grace of God that is revealed. He continues: 'That at least is my mind, and if the whole world agreed to condemn it or see nothing in it I should only tell them to take a generation and come to me again.' He knew that he was ahead of his time.

His reading of the story of the shipwreck draws upon the newspaper report, but his poem could not be more different from the journalism of that piece. The first part of the poem is about his own relationship with God, as seen in the opening lines:

Thou mastering me
God! giver of breath and bread;
World's strand, sway of the sea;
Lord of living and dead;
Thou hast bound bones & veins in me, fastened me flesh,
And after it almost unmade, what with dread,
Thy doing: and dost thou touch me afresh?
Over again I feel thy finger and find thee.

The second part turns to consider the nuns, especially the tall nun reported to have cried out 'O Christ come quickly' as the ship foundered:

Sister, a sister calling
A master, her master and mine! –
And the inboard seas run swirling and hawling;

The rash smart sloggering brine
Blinds her; but she that weather sees one thing, one;
Has one fetch in her: she rears herself to divine
Ears, and the call of the tall nun
To the men in the tops and the tackle rode over the storm's brawling.

After a dozen or more stanzas reflecting on the plight of the nuns, the poet gradually turns to consider his own life and the state of Britain. Earlier in the poem he had touched upon the politics that led to the nuns' expulsion: 'Rhine refused them.' The final stanza is a prophetic outburst about Britain in a language full of grace.

Dame, at our door
Drowned, and among our shoals,
Remember us in the roads, the heaven-haven of the Reward:
Our King back, Oh, upon English souls!
Let him easter in us, be a dayspring to the dimness of us,
    be a crimson-cresseted east,
More brightening her, rare-dear Britain, as his reign rolls,
Pride, rose, prince, hero of us, high-priest,
Our hearts' charity's hearth's fire, our thoughts' chivalry's throng's
    Lord.

This long poem telling the story of the shipwreck both reads the signs of the times and writes about them in a new language. The wreck is not only the ship, but also the society which had expelled the nuns from Germany and stripped rare-dear Britain of its fire and its Lord.

This is not a poem *about* grace; the language of the poem *is* grace. The truth of the signs of the times is revealed to the reader *in* the words, not *through* them. 'Let him easter in us' transforms Easter from a past event into a verb about a present experience. In describing the wreck of ship and society, Hopkins reads and writes grace, reaching beyond the good news/bad news split into the heart of the Easter mystery of death and new life.

Throughout 'The Wreck', the Easter mystery is explicitly revealed by Hopkins. But as his style developed, the Christian foundation of his language is more discreet, and the reader must work harder to see the mystery, just as the writer worked hard to see it and write it. This is the case with 'The Windhover'.

To Christ our Lord

I caught this morning morning's minion, king-
     dom of daylight's dauphin, dapple-dawn-drawn Falcon, in his riding
     Of the rolling level underneath him steady air, and striding
High there, how he rung upon the rein of a wimpling wing
In his ecstasy! Then off, off forth on swing,
     As a skate's heel sweeps smooth on a bow-bend: the hurl and gliding
     Rebuffed the big wind. My heart in hiding
Stirred for a bird, – the achieve of, the mastery of the thing!

There is so much new technique in this poem that it is dizzying to consider it all. And all these new linguistic devices have a dizzying effect on the reader, which is exactly the effect Hopkins intends. He is dizzy with looking up at the kestrel hovering above him and then suddenly swooping off in a new direction. This poetic form is not immediately intelligible on first reading, but its overall impact is greater than a simple description of a bird in flight.

The final part of the poem has a different focus, as the poet now speaks to 'thee', which takes us back to the opening dedication, 'To Christ our Lord'. The bird's beauty is now seen as the sign of 'my chevalier' or knight, who the dedication implies is Christ.

> Brute beauty and valour and act, oh, air, pride, plume, here
> Buckle! AND the fire that breaks from thee then, a billion
> Times told lovelier, more dangerous, O my chevalier!
>
> No wonder of it: sheer plod makes plough down sillion
> Shine, and blue-bleak embers, ah my dear,
> Fall, gall themselves, and gash gold-vermilion.

Those final three lines show the poet no longer looking up at the sky but down at the field, as a plodding ploughman creates a sillion, the slice of soil that is turned over by the plough, which can shine in sunlight when freshly cut. This he compares to the bleak embers of a fire that fall open to reveal red and gold. So too Christ's beauty breaks out, not only from the bird but also from the soil and the fire, from all of nature. This is a sacramental reading of nature and of life. To convey this, Hopkins must break and re-form ordinary language, so that words 'fall, gall themselves and gash' the visible world to reveal it as a place of grace.

Hopkins was conscious that what he wrote may not be accessible to others: 'Plainly if it is possible to express a subtle and recondite thought on a subtle and recondite subject in a subtle and recondite way and with great felicity and perfection, in the end, something must be sacrificed.' He goes on to say that the thing sacrificed 'may be the being at once, nay perhaps even the being without explanation at all, intelligible'. He concluded:

'The verses stand or fall by their simple selves.' Rarely has somebody been so conscious that they are crafting a new language out of the words and structures of ordinary language. This is the way the language of grace works: it is always seeking new expression.

The Swiss theologian Hans Urs von Balthasar offers an insight about the veiled theology of the poem:

> Christ's Cross is indeed not one historical
> fact among others; it is the fundamental
> presupposition of all natural processes which
> they intrinsically signify by pointing beyond
> themselves. 'The Windhover' allows this
> connection to appear expressly only in the
> dedication; in the poem itself the image must say
> all. (adapted from *The Glory of the Lord*, vol. 3)

Hopkins reads the signs of the world around him as revealing the mystery of Christ who is 'a billion times told lovelier, more dangerous' than even the dizzying kestrel. He shows how reading and writing the signs of the times has the same qualities as the reading and writing of the language of grace found in the texts considered in Chapters Four and Five: fresh, joyful, original descriptions that dive into life's beauty and cruelty to reveal the hope that is to be found there.

THE LANGUAGE OF SONG

If we turn from writing and reading to listening and speaking today, song is the art through which many people listen to and speak about the signs of the times. Thanks to modern technology of many different kinds, there is more global listening to songs and more global singing of those same songs than was imaginable a hundred years ago. Alongside live performances, electronic devices large and small make ours a world of song. This is itself a sign of the times, a sign perhaps of a universal desire for a language that offers beauty and inspiration, an implicit longing for the language of grace.

There are so many kinds of song, ranging from pop, soul, rock and folk to musicals, four-part motets and opera. I'll look at just three living song writers and performers: a leading boy band, a classical composer and a classical singer.

The President of South Korea introduced the 2021 General Assembly of the United Nations with a performance by BTS, a Korean boy band formed by a group of teenagers in 2010 who by the end of the decade had risen to international stardom on a colossal scale. ARMY is the name of their fandom, reckoned by commentators to be the largest group of music fans in the world. Some fans do not simply enjoy the band as their idols, but draw spiritual messages from the band's lyrics in albums such as *Love Yourself* and *Map of the Soul*. The latter sold over four million copies in advance of release and another four million within ten days of release in 2020. Their live performances are embedded in spectacular shows and made into music videos with high production values. This is a highly commercialized culture of entertainment that carries compassionate messages to many millions of young people.

Just as there is fool's gold, the base mineral that looks like gold, can we also say there is fool's grace? How can we distinguish real grace from fool's grace? Are the BTS lyrics, performances and videos the language of grace or not? I leave those with a real understanding of their music and culture to answer that question but, given the scale of this popular culture, it is certainly a question worth answering.

I turn instead to a musical world that is both more familiar to me and strikingly original. Sir James MacMillan is arguably Britain's greatest living composer of classical music. The breadth of his compositions is breathtaking, even if we just look at his choral works: church anthems, congregational settings of the Mass, a whole new *Christmas Oratorio*, settings of the Passion and of new secular texts. To listen to his choral music is to experience the language of grace in a style that brings together the ancient and the modern with refreshing and sometimes shocking originality. The themes of these works are spiritual and political, often combining the two, as in his *Cantos Sagrados*. 'In writing this work', he said,

> I wanted to compose something which was both timeless and contemporary, both sacred and secular. The title [Sacred Songs] is therefore slightly misleading, as the three poems are concerned with political repression in Latin America and are deliberately coupled with traditional religious texts to emphasize a deeper solidarity with the poor of that sub-continent.

MacMillan is a practising Catholic, and the choral music he composes is his language of grace, a creative expression both of what his faith tells him is life's purpose and of all that frustrates this purpose. His work is widely recognized as of the highest quality in both religious and secular circles. Once again, when expressed creatively and not in clichés, the language of grace speaks not only to people of faith but also to those who are spiritual even if not religious.

In addition to the established body of James MacMillan's compositions I want to explore the emerging work of Davone Tines, an African American singer trained in the classical tradition. He combines very different kinds of song, by a variety of composers, to create distinctive live performances. One such piece for voice and piano is *Recital No 1: Mass,* a 75-minute programme of songs that I heard recently. Each section began with an excerpt from one of the traditional parts of the Mass, sung in Latin to a simple modern setting. This was followed by a classical aria or spirituals or contemporary songs by Black composers.

Bach's beautiful aria of renewal from the *St Matthew Passion, 'Mache Dich Mein Herze Rein'* (Make my heart pure), was sung in an exuberant style of full-throated joy. A friend pointed out that this music is marked by Bach as a sarabande, a dance, and that Tines really made the music dance. Christ was not only being asked to make my heart pure; he was also being asked to dance in my heart! Then there was the gruelling Prelude to Julius Eastman's *The Holy Presence of Joan of Arc,* a litany of Joan's pleading as she faced execution, sung with such uncompromising repetition that I felt uncomfortable as the ten minutes of this section wore me down. And in between there were heart-rending spirituals: 'To a

Brown Girl, Dead' and a reworked version of 'Swing Low, Sweet Chariot'.

Tines was brought up Episcopalian and understands that tradition, but no longer identifies with any church. He describes the structure of this Mass as follows:

> identifying a problem, the *Kyrie* [Lord have mercy]; *Agnus Dei*: knowing that something has to be sacrificed in order to make change, because that's what change is – something goes away or changes; *Credo*: believing that change can happen. *Gloria* is rejoicing in the fact that that change has happened, or that there's the possibility of change. And *Sanctus* is an acknowledgement of how special the possibility of this process is, that there actually is some sort of road to move on from whatever tension they feel to a release.

Tines said he set out to disrupt what people expect from a recital, because he saw singers who followed a recital pattern of traditional pieces plus a concluding piece that delighted them personally. He noticed they usually sang the last piece best, so he decided to create a whole recital with pieces that delight him. By using sections of the Mass as the framework, he was connecting with a spiritual tradition that not only unifies the piece but also connects to the concerns he explores in the songs: injustice and violence, sacrifice and hope.

Recital No 1: Mass was not easy listening, but it was without doubt one man's expression, through Christian music, of his insight into life's meaning and purpose. Tines sings to promote justice and equality by weaving his understanding of life today out of the living tradition of Christian song. His creativity connects the classical tradition with African American spirituals and contemporary music to create something fresh, a language of grace that goes beyond the musical conventions he inherited.

Whether listening to MacMillan or Tines or following BTS, or indeed singing their music, we are touched by song and music as by no other language. A song can enter the heart and mind in a unique way, and is more memorable than a spoken text. As MacMillan observes: 'Through its directness and abstraction, music seems to have the ability to reach the soul and address the relationship between the human and the divine in a powerful, mysterious way.' He contrasts his own work with that of some contemporaries, such as Arvo Pärt, who go for a pure line of music, while his spirituality requires 'a commitment to human suffering ... my character and theological viewpoint call for conflict. After all, the heart of Christian thinking is the sacrificial story.' As we've been discovering throughout this book, the language of grace in all its forms describes the harsh realities of life as well as life's consolations. The language of grace is never saccharine.

What makes a great song is a question for musical experts. What makes a song a way of listening to and speaking about the signs of the times is a more focused question. A song can be a true speaking of the language of grace for our times when its lyrics open the hidden stream of grace that flows through life today. This has three dimensions: a celebration of the goodness of life, an expression of gratitude that this evokes, and an indication of the hard realities that block the flow of grace. For Christians this is the stream of God's life and love, but it is not necessary to name that life and love as God's for it to be from God. The quality of grace is not dependent on our naming it. Christians have the privilege of recognizing it as Christ's gift and the duty to celebrate it as such. This is the privilege and the duty of listening and speaking, writing and reading the signs of the times through which God's grace flows.

LANGUAGE THAT BUILDS CONSENSUS

The West is currently experiencing an acceleration of the collapse of its post-war consensus about everything from faith and morality to political and social norms. When the collapse began is a matter of controversy, but it became evident in the 1960s and has gained pace since the start of the new millennium. From the 1960s onwards, more and more people dropped inherited conventions of dress and lifestyle in favour of doing their own thing. The disappearance of some of these norms is beneficial, but there is little agreement about which ones are best kept and which should be abandoned – for example, whether the legal restrictions on drug use should be reformed as with the licensed sale of cannabis in some countries.

The principle that we can all do our own thing provided we don't harm others was for decades the conscious or unconscious moral principle of many people. It was always a weak principle because it begged two questions. What constitutes harm? Who are the others? For example, a man privately promises his dying mother that he will keep the family home and not sell it. After his mother dies, he does sell the home. Is breaking a promise harmful? To whom?

This principle has now collapsed altogether in the face of new ethical challenges. So I'll briefly look at them and consider how a language of grace needs to be developed to address the dilemmas posed by these realities. No attempt will be made to resolve the issues; instead I'll explore the language around them and how good language is vital to resolving them. I will be exploring new ways of speaking on controversial subjects, so I will be touching sensitive areas. The capacity for language to cause offence is very real, and I have tried to outline a gracious way of addressing such areas. This is not straightforward, so I hope the reader can accept that this is a search, not a final answer, and so forgive any phrases considered insensitive.

AUTHENTICITY

As socially accepted norms have faded and as the harm-to-others principle has proved an inadequate substitute, a new criterion for validating a person's choices has quietly established itself. A person's choice is now validated by the fact of the person choosing it. The act of choosing authenticates the choice and places it beyond challenge. Authenticity is its own validation.

For example, authenticity is a key part of the transgender rights debate. Trans men and women often say they have made an authentic choice of gender, irrespective of their biological sex. Some feminists challenge some aspects of their right to do this. They believe that, in some respects, gender identity does not always outweigh biological sex. On this view, people are free to choose their own gender lifestyle and have some legal protection for that but, so the argument goes, defining sexual identity solely by personal choice is unacceptable; it harms the identity of women and can compromise their safety in single-sex spaces, for example. Opponents of this view claim that such opinions disrespect trans people and leave them open to verbal and physical abuse. Freedom of speech, they say, cannot override freedom from harm. Here two harms are being pitched against one another. This is a serious disagreement, but it is not resolved by assertions.

If we accept authentic assertion as a truth criterion then discussion and discernment cease. Those who seek change in social norms will inevitably face the risk of being challenged. Similarly, those who oppose the change need to listen at depth to those proposing change, not simply to counter their arguments but to understand the heart and mind of the other sympathetically. Assertion and counter assertion do not reveal where the grace in the situation is to be found. Deep listening and sensitive speaking are the steps along the path to consensus.

A fine example of reconciling opposing views on sexuality in a different context was given in a brief dialogue between Pope Francis and the gay comedian Stephen K. Amos. The BBC TV programme *Pilgrimage* has had several series with a group of pilgrims of diverse beliefs following a traditional pilgrim route. In *Pilgrimage: The Road to Rome* the climax of the journey was a private audience with Pope Francis during which the pilgrims could ask the Pope anything they liked. Stephen told the Pope he'd gone on the pilgrimage looking for answers and faith but that 'as a gay man, I don't feel accepted.' The Pope replied: 'To emphasize the adjective over the noun is not good. Each of us is a person and has dignity. If this person is like this or has a tendency like that, it does not change their dignity. Those who want to choose or discard people because of the adjective do not have a human heart.' As the audience ended, the Pope embraced Stephen, who was in tears. When asked for his reaction afterwards, Stephen said simply: 'His candid and honest response blew my mind. That's what I've been searching for, for a long time.' This was the language of grace in word and gesture on both sides of the dialogue, reaching across divided opinions to a new place of meeting.

THE PAST

History and its interpretation have always been debated, but in recent years this has become a contentious issue in daily life across the world, leading to mass protests and the removal or destruction of monuments. In 2020, the Black Lives Matter movement sparked debates in many countries not only about continuing racial prejudice but also about monuments that celebrated men who had made fortunes out of the slave trade. Here in England, for example, Edward Colston in Bristol and Sir John Cass in London were active in the slave trade in the early eighteenth century. Both were also wealthy philanthropists who endowed charities that continue to do good work today. As a result of their philanthropy, they had statues and institutions named after them, but by the end of 2021 the institutions were renamed and many statues of them had been removed or destroyed. This movement had been building for some time, as the case of Colston illustrates; the renaming of Bristol institutions bearing his name was already underway from 2017. The toppling of Colston's statue by a crowd in 2020 was the very public culmination of a long process.

One of the difficulties in speaking about Black Lives Matter is that it is both a specific organization and a wider uncontrolled movement. Those who created events within the wider movement sometimes disagreed with the policies of the organization. And then there were simply local conversations about race between people who support neither the organization nor the movement but who were simply responding to the news coverage. Families with a history of being enslaved felt able to describe the pain and sorrow of their past and of their present. I found myself asking friends of colour what prejudice they had experienced; they told me some appalling stories, and then added that I was the first white person ever to ask them about it. Away from the big events, this was a moment of grace on many levels; people found a language of grace that enabled them to confront the evils of the past, but in such a way as to foster grace in the future.

Yet some other ways of looking at the past have the opposite effect. I have no hesitation in affirming the reality of climate change and the human factors that drive it. But there is a way of describing this that sounds misanthropic, disdainful of past human societies as well as contemptuous of the present.

In this way of speaking, the past is no longer just a foreign country where they do things differently; it has become a shameful way of life that created what is seen as the present toxic world of racial oppression and climate disaster. In a word, the past is a disgrace. That we need to take action to correct racial prejudice and environmental degradation is beyond doubt, but I question the need to demonize the past in order to achieve this.

Take the parallel of a human being guilty of a crime. Shouting at the criminal and telling him his past life is a disgrace may be a really important step in restorative justice for the victim and for society's desire to see retribution. But it isn't going to change the past or create a better future for the perpetrator of the crime and society at large. To do that we need places like HMP Grendon, one of just two specialist prisons in England and Wales that function as therapeutic communities. I was once asked to contribute to a conference for some of the 200 prisoners there and glimpsed the extraordinary work undertaken in this prison.

Those serving long sentences elsewhere may be recommended for transfer to Grendon. There they can participate in long-term group therapy to develop their relationship skills and improve their mental health. Their past is neither forgotten nor forgiven, but the focus of their life at Grendon is developing a better future.

So too with racial prejudice and climate degradation; these hard realities must not be trivialized, but viewing history exclusively through the destructive forces of the past runs the risk of making contemporary problems seem insurmountable; the past is considered so terrible that the present is beyond redemption. Instead of framing the past as simply a disgrace, we need to reframe past errors so that they can form the basis for a better future. This does not involve excusing the past, but it does involve understanding the specific causes of past horrors as well as celebrating those who began the work of remedying them and focusing on extending the remedies in ways that include people of differing opinions.

Context is the key here, and reframing is the process of putting a new context around a problem to see it in a new light. Instead of labelling the past as simply a disaster, reframing the past enables us to see both light and shade in the complex history that has led to contemporary problems. This is language work that aims to find both the grace and the disgrace in the past with a view to creating a more gracious future. One of the best ways to reframe social problems in this way is an imaginatively run museum.

The Birmingham Civil Rights Institute (BCRI) in Alabama is a shining example of what I mean. It describes its mission as 'To enlighten each generation about civil and human rights by exploring our common past and working together in the present to build a better future.' The whole tone of the place is forward-looking even as the shocking events of the past are recounted. I visited it as part of a leadership workshop for abbots being held at a nearby monastery. I couldn't imagine why this visit was included in the programme, but once there I was bowled over. We were greeted by guides proudly wearing 'I walked with MLK' badges, we watched a film describing the Jim Crow laws, we saw newsreel footage of dogs and fire hoses turned on black children, we sat in part of a segregated restaurant that had been moved to the museum; but we were also walked through the development of civil rights and the desegregation of schools; the guides told us of the progress and the setbacks in establishing civil rights in the US. Here was a context that pulled no punches about the past, but was also a stepping-stone to a better future and a place of hope. The community that supports the BCRI embodies a language of grace founded on but not defined by disgraceful past events. This is how we can make the past a place of grace for the future.

As the leader of a Catholic religious congregation some of whose members have abused children, I know that the Church has barely begun to learn how to generate a renewed language of grace in the wake of the clerical abuse crisis. How to reframe such a horrendous past to build a better future for all is still unclear, and we need new reforming saints to lead this process. This abuse is not all in the past because, as I described in an earlier chapter, the impact of abuse destroys trust and lasts a lifetime for those who survive it. The task of rebuilding trust in the Church is one that affects me deeply and has dominated my life in recent years. I have offered public apologies to those abused, but that is not enough. I have tried to do more through, for example, working with a university project analysing the causes of abuse in the Church and privately by staying in touch with some survivors who wish to do so as they seek to rebuild their lives. An important aspect of the wider Church task is the reform begun by Pope

Francis by setting up the Pontifical Commission for the Protection of Minors and by meeting survivors himself both at home and on his travels. By seeking to reduce clericalism and giving a greater role to lay women and men, he hopes to create a more trustworthy Church that can address past failures and look to the future with hope.

THE FUTURE

Just as there is a danger that focusing on past wrongs can lead to seeing the past as a disgrace, so too identifying future risks can lead to seeing the future as a disaster. Again, museums provide a healthy antidote to such a negative understanding. Climate museums are in their infancy in the UK and in the US but, like the BCRI, the two already in existence are pursuing a positive agenda about the future. Neither climate museum has a permanent home, so instead they create temporary spaces where people can devise and implement a better environmental future. I particularly like the self-description of the Climate Museum UK. It is neither utopian nor dystopian in its view of the future, and describes its approach as Possitopian. The emphasis is on developing conversations around science and art, lifestyle and choices. From these scientific and artistic conversations new projects emerge. This is a helpful antidote to seeing conversations as just more blah, blah, blah! Good conversations are the foundations of a better future. They can of course become a substitute for a better future, but these museums show how well-managed conversations are a key part of action. They do not minimize the enormity of the challenge, but neither do they catastrophize it.

This book began with my family's history of emigrating from Australia to England in the 1950s. We were brought up to cheer for Australia in sport and to share the joys of pavlova and barbecues with a Britain still recovering from Spam and rationing. We were proudly Australian. As an ethnically white family, we never experienced the racial prejudice experienced by African and Asian migrants. Yet we were perhaps more conscious of such prejudice than many people. So it has been a wonderful discovery for me to find the Migration Museum in London. Founded in the early 2010s by Barbara Roche, a former government immigration minister, the museum began by creating temporary exhibitions that celebrate the story of immigration to Britain. It now has a more permanent home in South London. At a time when attitudes to migration are so often negative, this museum is another sign of grace where people are seeking a better language with which to address what is undeniably one of the great political challenges of our time. The mass migration of peoples is here to stay for the foreseeable future, and it poses profound socio-economic challenges which require not simply assertions but a careful language with which to find solutions. As with the issues described in the previous section, so with immigration, the language we use to describe it makes things either better or worse. This can be derided as political correctness, but to do that misses the point: the way we think is expressed in and shaped by language. Language is the portal through which we experience life. And that's why it matters.

'Correcting' someone's language is not the intention; the purpose of good language is to help us all to handle a demanding aspect of life creatively and joyfully.

The museums mentioned above and other such places are temples of grace run by communities developing a new language within which to reframe contemporary issues. They show that there is an alternative to the pervasive view that the past is a disgrace and the future will be a disaster. That narrative is not only untrue but also mentally unhealthy, because it fosters mistrust rather than seeking to restore trust. It is all too easy to foster mistrust as the answer to contemporary problems. Mistrust of what is alien: foreigners, other religions, refugees. Mistrust of what is familiar: politicians, business leaders, the media. Mistrust of the past and of the future. It is an easy tactic to foster original mistrust and turn it into a strategy that goes something like, 'Keep out the foreigners, don't listen to mainstream media, replace corrupt politicians,' or, 'Business leaders are only interested in money, politicians lie, civil disobedience is the only solution.'

The examples of listening and speaking, writing and reading described in the previous chapters show how the creators of the language of grace offer an alternative path. It is the much more demanding path of trust building, and they often pay a high personal price for their creativity. They persevere because they believe the grace of God can flow through the fertile language they have generated. Some, such as Teresa of Avila, were despised by those who saw themselves as guardians of orthodoxy. It is wonderful that those detractors are now forgotten, and that Teresa is recognized as Saint

Teresa and a doctor of the Church. Today there are secular orthodoxies as well as religious ones with some equally fierce guardians. I believe that the language of grace pulls through despite its detractors, that grace is a real quality which has an eternal shelf life. By contrast, the language that fosters mistrust eventually withers, but can do untold damage before it dies. To overcome mistrust between nations, communities and individuals, we need artisans of the language of grace.

A FINAL EXERCISE

There are no detailed exercises to conclude this final chapter. I simply invite you to be aware of how people speak and write when they are discussing contemporary issues that evoke strong opinions on all sides. Then ask one simple question: does their way of speaking build trust? Finally, take one practical step yourself, which should flow naturally from the previous exercises: when you are part of such a discussion, try to speak the language of grace.

Conclusion

DEAD LANGUAGE

Languages can die. If a language has no written form, when the last native speaker of a language dies, then the language dies too. For native English speakers, the idea of a language dying may seem inconceivable. After all, an estimated two billion people speak English with some degree of competence. By contrast, data gathered by the Summer Institute of Linguistics in 1999 records that, out of over 6,000 languages, half have fewer than 100,000 speakers, and 500 of these have fewer than 100 speakers. No wonder, then, that experts predict half of the world's 6,000 languages will die out by the end of this century.

Such statistics recall similar predictions about environmental loss and extinction rates in the natural world. The two are connected: small native communities with their unique languages can be wiped out by natural disasters or by colonial takeover of their lands.

Yet there are also success stories of languages being not only saved from extinction but also restored to the mainstream of modern life. Wales is a good example; at the start of the twentieth century, the number of Welsh speakers was in sharp decline, with children punished for speaking Welsh at school. But cultural and political action turned this round, so that today Welsh is widely used as the medium of instruction in many schools.

LIVING LANGUAGE

The way to sustain the living language of grace is illustrated by another personal experience, this time after I had entered the monastery at Worth Abbey and been ordained a priest. In the 1960s, Worth had founded a mission in Peru; heroically, if unwisely, the mission began in a remote Andean valley, but in the 1980s moved to a shanty town on the outskirts of Lima. I was not posted there but, as I spoke Spanish, I was occasionally sent there to assist with the work for a month, allowing one of the other priests to take a break. In 1988, I was privileged to attend a summer school of theology in Lima and listened to Fr Gustavo Gutiérrez, the foremost exponent of what became known as the Theology of Liberation. Those participating in the summer school were mainly young, coming from what the Peruvian Church calls 'popular sectors', the shanty towns made up mainly of poor or destitute families. Gutiérrez posed a question that struck me powerfully. He asked: 'How can we speak of the God of life in the midst of a reality of death?'

Of course, the doctrines of the Church were well known to Gutiérrez, who has a doctorate in theology from the University of Lyon. He could have plucked any number of doctrines off the library shelf and expounded them. So what was he actually asking? The question he posed was, 'How can we speak?' – what language to use? He was searching for a language about the action of God, a language of grace, that would not only be true to Christian doctrine, but also address the 'reality' facing many members of his youthful audience. 'Reality' is a key word here. The reality of those in front of Gutiérrez was poverty and death; doing theology from this starting point led to the development of the 'fundamental option for the poor', which in turn became the main orientation of the Latin American Church's teaching of the Christian faith and how it is to be lived.

Gutiérrez and others like him developed this theology in such a way that it transformed the Latin American Church. Pope Benedict XVI criticized Marxist means to achieve justice for the poor within this theology, but nevertheless affirmed an option for the poor as part of traditional Catholic doctrine. In the teaching and work of Pope Francis, we see the working out of the current Pope's version of this language, which he has called the Theology of the People. Finding 'how to speak about the God of life' makes sense only if it is connected to the 'reality' of daily life. That is why language matters. It both describes and channels life-changing grace.

In this sense, the Christian faith is language work. In this language work, theologians go into the heart of life, looking for the traces of grace to be found there, just like those writing Catholic novels; both seek 'how to speak' in a way that lifts doctrine off the shelf and rediscovers it in 'reality'. This creative process in both theology and literature is about starting with experience. It attracts criticism both from secular people who do not acknowledge the existence of God and his grace, as well as from religious fundamentalists who want to confine grace to the shelf of doctrinal religious terms. The language of grace is an increasingly dead language in Western society, unknown to most and restricted to the custody of those who would keep it in the deep freeze of so-called traditional orthodoxy. This book is offered to those who want to explore how grace can be a living language.

Bibliography

CHAPTER 1

Iain McGilchrist's website, https://channelmcgilchrist.com,
explains his insights about the brain and our culture.

Aquinas, Thomas, *Summa Theologiae,* First Part of the Second
Part, 109–14, especially 110.

Ernst, Cornelius (1974), *The Theology of Grace*, Montréal:
Fides.

McGilchrist, Iain (2009), *The Master and His Emissary: The
Divided Brain and the Making of the Western World*, New
Haven: Yale UP.

Robinson, Marilynne (2010), *Absence of Mind.* New Haven:
Yale UP.

CHAPTER 2

Crystal, David (2007), *How Language* Works. London: Penguin.

Endo, Shusaku (2016), *Silence,* translated by William Johnston,
introduction by Martin Scorsese. London: Picador.

Ivens SJ, Michael (2016), *Understanding the Spiritual Exercises:
Text and Commentary: A Handbook for Retreat Directors.*
Leominster: Gracewing. NB: for retreat directors.

Malouf, David (1985), 'The Only Speaker of his Tongue' in
Antipodies. London: Chatto & Windus.

The Rule of St Benedict (1980). Collegeville, MN: Liturgical Press.

Video: https://vimeo.com/110415962, A short video about the Kumla Monastery.

CHAPTER 3

De Troyes, Chrétien (2004), *The Story of the Grail* in *Arthurian Romances*. London: Penguin.

Tyler, Peter (2013), 'The Psychology of Vocation: Nurturing the Grail Quest' in ed. Jamison, *The Disciples' Call*. London: Bloomsbury.

https://courtyardproject.org.uk for information about Courtyard

CHAPTER 4

Clayton, Ewan (2013), *The Golden Thread: The Story of Writing*. London: Atlantic Books.

interview in *Financial Times,* 13 September 2013.

St Teresa of Avila (1980), *Her Life*, in trans. K. Kavanaugh and O. Rodriguez, *The Collected Works*. Washington, DC: ICS Publications.

St John of the Cross (1991), *Poems* in trans. K. Kavanaugh and O. Rodriguez, *The Collected Works*, revised 1991. Washington, DC: ICS Publications. This is the translation used here.

Poems, translated into poetry by Roy Campbell (1960). London: Penguin.

CHAPTER 5

Hugh of St Victor (2018), *Didascalicon*. Reprint of 1961 edition. London: Forgotten Books.

Illich, Ivan (1996), *In the Vineyard of the Text: A Commentary to*

Hugh's Didascalicon. Chicago: University of Chicago Press.
Robinson, Marilynne (2006), *Gilead*. London: Virago.
(2020), *Jack*. London: Virago.
St Augustine of Hippo, *Confessions* (multiple editions).

CHAPTER 6

Hopkins, Gerard Manley (2008), *Poems and* Prose. London: Penguin.
Von Balthasar, Hans Urs (1986), *The Glory of the Lord*, vol. 3. Edinburgh: T. & T. Clark.
'On Sir James MacMillan': programme notes on the UK Premiere of *Christmas Oratorio* by Anthony Fiumara. London, 2020.